VIM & VINEGAR

ALSO BY MELODIE MOORE

Smart Solutions for Saving Money and Time
Smart Cents

VIM & VINEGAR

MELODIE MOORE

HarperPerennial

A Division of HarperCollins*Publishers*

HarperCollins books may be purchased for educational, business, or sales promotional use. For information please write: Special Markets Department, HarperCollins Publishers, Inc., 10 East 53rd Street, New York, NY 10022.

FIRST EDITION

Designed by Helene Wald Berinsky

Library of Congress Cataloging-in-Publication Data

Moore, Melodie
        Vim & vinegar / Melodie Moore. — 1st ed.
                p.   cm.
        Includes bibliographical references and index.
                ISBN 0–06–095223–7
    1. House cleaning.   2. Vinegar.   3. Cookery (Vinegar)
                I. Title.
                TX324.M63   1997
        664'.55—dc21   96-45253

97 98 99 00 01 ❖/RRD 10 9 8 7 6 5 4 3 2 1

■ CONTENTS ■

■ INTRODUCTION ■

I have been a fan of vinegar all my life. As a young child and a teenager I practically lived in the sun during the summer because I was a member of the swim team. As a fair-skinned redhead I was constantly battling a sunburn. I found out at an early age that after exposure to the sun I could avoid sunburn pain by rubbing vinegar on my skin before the burn appeared. If this was its only use, I would still think that vinegar is a miracle product, but over the years I have found an almost unlimited number of practical uses for vinegar. As the editor of *Tightwad Living* magazine, I frequently publish money saving tips and formulas that include vinegar. Subscribers from every part of the country send in thousands of tips each year, many of which include the "miracle" product vinegar.

The origin of vinegar was never specifically noted in any historical record. Among the oldest of foods and medicines known to humans, its discovery most likely occurred about ten thousand years ago, when wine was discovered, since vinegar is essentially spoiled wine. In the centuries before wine production was perfected, much of the wine accidentally turned into vinegar. In fact the French wine port of Orleans became known for its vinegar in the fourteenth century because of the frequency of this occurrence. There is some debate over the origin of the word *vinegar*. Some say the word came from the French *vinaigre—vin* (wine) plus *aigre* (sour), while others say it came from the Latin *vinum* (wine) plus *acer* (sharp).

Vinegar is a wonderful cleaning agent. You can use it to clean anything from greasy countertops to carpet stains to miniblinds. It is one of the lowest-priced multiuse products you can buy. The most common use of vinegar either by businesses or homemakers is in the making of salad dressing. Vinegar can be found in approximately 98 percent of American homes. For decades, vinegar sales remained constant and were limited mainly to distilled vinegar and apple cider vinegar. Since 1986, however, interest in different types of vinegars and in flavored vinegars has caused an increase of about 10 percent.

Vinegar is low in calories and carbohydrates. It contains small amounts of calcium, phosphorus, iron, and lots of potassium. A cup of apple cider vinegar is 98.8 percent water, has 34 calories, a trace of protein, and no fat.

Most of the thousands of years vinegar has been in existence, its many uses have not been exploited. The new popularity of vinegar stems from its ability to add wonderful flavors to food without adding extra fat and calories, to aid in numerous household chores, and to enhance body treatments. With many forms and uses, vinegar perks up our favorite foods and improves our homes and lives.

Vinegar is made by fermenting a sweet juice. The juice becomes wine or cider, which is put aside to ferment a second time until the alcohol mixes with oxygen in the air, changing it into acetic acid and water. The acetic acid is what gives vinegar its tart and sour taste. There are many different types of vinegar available. The best vinegars to use for cleaning are distilled white vinegar or apple cider vinegar. White distilled vinegar is not often used in cooking since it has a sharp taste. More expensive vinegars such as wine vinegar and balsamic vinegar are nice for cooking but are not suitable for cleaning tasks. Most grocery stores and some discount chains (such as Wal-Mart or K mart) stock low-priced gallon jugs of vinegar. A gallon jug often costs about the same as a small bottle. After reading this book you'll see why you need the large economy size.

The strength of vinegar is important. All varieties of vinegar contain about 4 to 7 percent acetic acid, with 5 percent being the most common amount. You can buy stronger solutions of acetic acid at drugstores but not without a prescription. If you'd like a stronger solution than your bottled vinegar provides, boil the vinegar, which will cause some of the water to evaporate, thereby increasing the percentage of the remaining acetic acid. For example, a 16-ounce bottle of vinegar evaporated down to 8 ounces, would raise the acetic acid from 5 percent to about 10 percent. Just remember, the stronger the acetic acid, the more powerful the solution and the more dangerous it is to handle. For most cleaning jobs, a standard 5 percent acetic acid solution works just great and will, in fact, require some dilution with water.

Vinegar is a vital ingredient to most kitchens; without vinegar there would be no pickles, mustard, mayonnaise, or many other products we use every day. Every country around the world has in some way developed its own special way of using vinegar. In England "fish and chips" are served with malt vinegar. Pickled sausage and pickled eggs are found in all corners of the world. Pickled herring from Scandinavia is a favorite specialty item here in the United States and in many other countries. Relishes and pickled cucumbers date back to Roman times. Vinegar is listed as an ingredient in recipes for cakes, pies, candies, jellies, bread, pastries, sauces, condiments, marinades, soups, stews, and drinks. Vinegar is much more than just an ingredient in salad dressing. It has in one form or another become a beloved staple.

Although commercial vinegar is inexpensive, you may want to try making your own. It is easy and fun to do at home (see page 94). You won't have to spend a fortune to start this hobby, and you end up with a very useful product. You can make an endless supply of vinegars specially designed to suit your taste. Give vinegar making a try, I think you will enjoy it.

The History of Vinegar

Vinegar was probably discovered over ten thousand years ago, when our ancestors found that wine exposed to the air would turn sour, thereby creating vinegar. Vinegar was first mentioned for its medicinal value in a tablet in Babylonia about seven thousand years ago. In 400 B.C. Hippocrates, known as the father of medicine, treated patients with vinegar, making it one of the world's first medicines. For "feminine" disorders, he recommended drinking a mixture of vinegar, honey, and pepper. An ancient Assyrian tablet prescribed vinegar for relieving earaches, and ancient Persian physicians recommended a drink of vinegar, lime juice, and sour fruit juice to help prevent obesity. Early Roman, Greek, and Asian physicians used vinegar to reduce bile and treat scurvy and digestive problems.

The ancient Romans and Greeks are known to have kept large quantities of vinegar in their cellars. They used vinegar in the kitchen to steep vegetables and marinate meat to tenderize it and add flavor. They also made pickles and preserved herbs, flowers, and vegetables with vinegar. Sweet-and-sour dishes, especially meat cooked in honey and vinegar and fruits and vegetables preserved in vinegar, were enjoyed in other ancient civilizations.

Throughout biblical times, vinegar was used to treat infections and wounds. Jesus was offered vinegar to drink on his way to Calvary, and was punished with a vinegar-soaked sponge while on the cross. The Book of Ruth in the Old Testament records that bowls filled with vinegar were placed on tables for dipping bread during meals. Diners soaked their stale bread in vinegar to freshen it. Since biblical times, workers have made their own kind of Gatorade with vinegar and salt water to keep energy levels up while toiling in the hot sun. Vinegar is mentioned in the Bible almost as many times as wine. There is even a Bible that was popularly known as the Vinegar Bible. Printed at Oxford, England, about 1717, it was named after a misprinted heading in the Gospel of Luke—"The Parable of the Vinegar" instead of "The Parable of the Vineyard."

Vinegar has played many interesting roles throughout history. The Roman army that once conquered much of the known world relied heavily on a vinegar "cocktail" to help them survive climatic changes and combat stress. Roman soldiers also used fire and vinegar alternately to force large rocks to expand in order to break their way through the Alps. The duc de Meilleraye, grand master of the artillery under Louis the XIII of France, charged the government 1.3 million francs for the vinegar used to cool his armies' cannons during battle. It is said that Cleopatra, queen of Egypt, dissolved a pearl or string of pearls in a glass of vinegar so she could win a bet that she could eat a meal with the value of a million sisterces, which was equal to several years' wages for the average workman during that time. She simply drank the glass of vinegar that had dissolved the pearls. You can see how this works at home without ruining your jewelry by dropping a bit of milk into vinegar. Milk and pearls contain calcium, which cannot withstand vinegar's acid.

During the Black Death, in the Middle Ages, bands of outlaws were able to steal from the dead and dying without getting sick by first dousing themselves with a mixture that came to be known as thieves vinegar or four thieves vinegar to protect themselves from the germs. Recipes for the mixture vary, but the generally accepted ingredients include leaves of rosemary, rue, sage, mint, and woodworm, plus lavender flowers and camphor gum. Other ingredients that may have been included are calamus root, cinnamon, cloves, nutmeg, and garlic.

Vinegar has been used as a food preservative. Our ancestors, who did not have the luxury of a refrigerator or freezer, had to either eat an entire animal in one sitting or find a way to preserve the meat to prevent spoilage. Soaking foods in vinegar solutions, or "pickling," in addition to smoking and salting, were ways that foods were preserved. The acidic nature of vinegar slows the growth of harmful bacteria in foods.

By the thirteenth century, Parisian street vendors were selling vinegar in a wide selection of flavors, including clove, chicory, fennel, garlic, ginger, mustard, raspberry, and truffle. Pepper vinegar was particularly popular during the Middle Ages because wine or vinegar that contained pepper was not charged an import tax when brought into Paris.

Once the industrial era began gearing up in the eighteenth century, cities throughout Europe grew full of people. To counteract the stench of raw sewage on the streets, as indoor plumbing was not yet common, people would walk or ride through Paris and London with sponges soaked in vinegar held to their noses. They preferred the smell of pungent vinegar to that of the raw sewage. Women carried these vinegar-dipped sponges in little silver boxes, and men stored them in special compartments in the heads of their walking canes.

During the American Civil War, thousands of lives were saved by using vinegar as a disinfectant and healing agent for battle wounds. Indeed, for centuries medical textbooks have listed ways to use vinegar. These uses include everything from keeping a sharp mind to purifying the waters of the body and to easing pain and alleviating dozens of other ailments. Modern laboratory analysis verifies the antibacterial and antiseptic properties of vinegar. Many of the old-time uses are just as applicable now as they were centuries ago.

In the United States in the eighteenth and nineteenth centuries, drinks combining fruit juice or water and fruit-flavored vinegar came to be known as switchels or shrubs. These drinks were used by laborers for refreshment during haying and harvesting.

Inexpensive, tasty, and natural, vinegar is much more than sour wine; it is nothing short of a modern-day miracle product!

VINEGAR TIPS FOR AROUND THE HOUSE

The mildly acidic nature of vinegar makes it useful for a wide range of cleaning jobs and other daily chores around the house. A gallon of distilled white or apple cider vinegar is inexpensive, and it has no noxious fumes or unhealthy additives. Vinegar can replace a number of bottles and boxes of cleaning supplies found under your kitchen sink or in the pantry. Vinegar is the best choice for those concerned about saving money and protecting the environment from harmful chemicals. Use inexpensive distilled white vinegar or apple cider vinegar for these projects; save the good stuff for cooking and home remedies.

When a cleaning job is tough enough to require a cleaner as strong as household ammonia or even bleach, try using vinegar first. Vinegar can accomplish many of the jobs that are traditionally assigned to bleach or ammonia and saves you from worrying about dangerous fumes. It's the safe, low-cost alternative. When doing routine cleaning chores, always be careful: a mixture of chlorine bleach and household ammonia creates a toxic gas. Even ammonia by itself can be toxic if you breathe it, so make sure that you have adequate ventilation when you do use it.

General Household Uses

UNCLOG DRAINS.

Pour ½ cup of baking soda followed by a cup of vinegar into the drain. Wait until it foams up; rinse it down with a gallon or two of hot tap water. Wait for about five minutes, then flush the drain with a gallon or two of cold tap water. This helps speed up a slow drain and leaves it smelling fresh. For best results, do this about once a month.

CLEAN TOUGH JOBS.

For really tough jobs, such as cleaning ceramic tiles, radiators, air vents, or dirty shower stalls, use ¼ cup baking soda in a gallon of very warm water with ½ cup vinegar and 1 cup clear ammonia. Wear rubber gloves and clean in a well-ventilated area.

CLEAN HUMIDIFIER FILTER.

To clean a foam humidifier or air-conditioner filter, take the filter out of the grill and soak it in a solution of half vinegar and half warm water. Clean the filter often, especially if someone in the house smokes. If you clean the filter regularly, about one hour of soaking will get it clean. If the filter is very dirty, let it soak several hours or overnight. Just squeeze the filter dry when it's clean.

CEILING FAN CLEANER.

Keep ceiling fan blades, air-conditioning grills, and exhaust fan grills dust free by wiping with full-strength white vinegar to cut the grease and dirt. This will keep them clean and facilitate the circulation of fresh air.

CLEAN/DEODORIZE MATTRESSES.

When small children or pets have an accident on a mattress, wash with a vinegar-and-water solution to take away the stain. Then fill a saucer with vinegar and set it in the room to eliminate the odor.

FRESHEN ROOMS.

To absorb stale, smoky odors, place a bowl of vinegar in an out-of-the-way place. To make the whole room smell better, put ½ cup vinegar, 2 cloves, and 1 teaspoon cinnamon into a small glass jar. Place the jar into the microwave on high for about 1 minute. Place the jar in the room, and it will absorb odors rather than just covering them up like a commercial air freshener.

ABSORB ODORS.

If the inside of an old box, foot locker, or car trunk smells, moisten a piece of bread with vinegar and leave it inside overnight to absorb the odor.

ELIMINATE MOTHBALL ODOR.

To get rid of mothball odor in a chest of drawers, scrub the inside of each drawer with a solution of half rubbing alcohol and half white vinegar. Remove the drawers and scrub the inside of the chest. Be sure to wipe down all surfaces. Mothball odor can be very persistent, and you may have to do this twice to completely eliminate the odor. If weather permits, do this outside and let the chest and drawers dry out in the sunlight.

MAKE PLASTIC ANTISTATIC.

Vinegar decreases static and keeps dust off plastic and vinyl surfaces. Wipe upholstery with a cloth dampened with a vinegar-water solution. Add a cup of vinegar to rinse water when laundering plastic curtains or tablecloths to help eliminate static and keep dust off.

CLEAN VENETIAN OR MINIBLINDS.

Put on an old pair of white cotton gloves and dampen the glove fingers in a mixture of half vinegar and half hot water. Rub your fingers over each slat of the blinds to remove dust and dirt. If you don't have an old pair of white gloves, use an old white sock instead.

WASH WINDOWS.

The absolute best way to clean windows is to dip old newspapers (black-and-white pages only) into a solution of half vinegar and half water. Wipe the glass with the wet newspapers until the glass is almost dry, then shine with dry newspapers or a soft cloth (like an old diaper or thin towel). The combination of vinegar and newspapers can't be beat (and neither can their price!).

CLEAN FIREPLACES.

To clean the brick or quarry tiles around a fireplace, dip a brush in white vinegar and scrub quickly. Use a soft towel or sponge to quickly blot up the moisture. Rinse with clean water.

CLEAN FIREPLACE GLASS.

Remove smoke stains on glass enclosures with a solution of ½ cup vinegar in 1 gallon warm water. Add 1 tablespoon clear ammonia. Spray on the glass or wipe it on with a cloth. Rinse with warm water and dry with a clean cloth.

CLEAN BRICK FLOORS.

Damp-mop a brick floor with a solution of one gallon of water and one cup of white vinegar. The floor will glisten without being polished.

REMOVE MILDEW.

Use vinegar at full strength for heavy mildew stains or mixed with water for light mildew stains. This procedure works for clothing, furniture, bathroom fixtures, shower curtains, painted surfaces, among others.

CLEAN BRASS, BRONZE, AND COPPER.

Mix vinegar with baking soda or salt to make a paste. Rub onto metal surfaces. Once the tarnish is removed, rinse with clean water. To keep copper pans shiny, wipe with a solution of vinegar and salt after each use.

CLEAN CHROME AND STAINLESS STEEL FIXTURES.
The best way to clean chrome fixtures is to spray lightly with vinegar. Polish to a shine with a dry cloth.

CLEAN COINS.
If you have some dirty old coins that you want clean and shiny again, soak them in vinegar and water overnight. When you rinse them off the next day, you'll see a dramatic difference. You can clean a whole coin collection easily.

REMOVE BALLPOINT PEN MARKS ON WALLS.
To remove ballpoint pen marks on painted walls and woodwork, dab the marks with distilled white vinegar. Blot frequently.

REMOVE CANDLE WAX.
To remove candle wax from a wood finish, first soften the wax by blowing it with warm air from a hair dryer. Then remove most of the wax with paper towels. Wash down the surface with a solution of half vinegar and half water to remove the remaining wax.

CLEAN BOOK COVERS.
To clean a cloth or vinyl book cover, wipe with a cloth dampened in a solution of one part vinegar and two parts water.

MAKE PRICE TAGS AND DECALS DISAPPEAR.
Apply full-strength vinegar directly on top and around the edges to remove price tags or decals from any surface. Give the vinegar time to soak in and then gently scrape it off. An old credit card is perfect for scraping off the sticky remains. Apply more vinegar to remove all traces of the decal.

CLEAN SILVER RINGS.
To clean silver rings and other silver objects, soak them in a solution of ½ cup vinegar and 2 tablespoons baking soda for two hours. Rinse with water and shine with a dry cloth. This will make dull and dark silver pieces look shiny and new.

DISSOLVE GLUE.
Many glues can be dissolved by applying a coat of vinegar and letting it soak for a few minutes.

MAKE WRAPPING TAPE ADHERE BETTER.
Add a few drops of vinegar to the water used to moisten wrapping tape, and it will stick to the package easily.

REACH CRACKS AND CREVICES.
Use a cotton swab dipped in white vinegar to clean small areas between blender and telephone buttons, in camera and sewing machine crevices, and other small spots.

WASH SOILED HANDS.
Heavily soiled hands can be cleaned and conditioned at the same time. Simply scrub hands with a paste made of cornmeal that has been moistened with apple cider vinegar. Rinse with cool water and pat dry. You'll remove all the dirt and grime, and your hands will feel very soft.

▪ Vinegar on Furniture and Wood ▪

POLISH FURNITURE.
Wipe furniture with a clean, soft cloth moistened with a mixture of 3 tablespoons vinegar and 1 quart water. This also removes cloudy film from varnished surfaces. Rub with grain of the wood. Polish with a soft, dry cloth.

DETER WOODWORMS.
Make a furniture polish and woodworm deterrent in one by combining 5 ounces linseed oil, 5 ounces turpentine, 2 ounces vinegar, and 2 ounces rubbing alcohol. Shake well; apply with a clean, soft cloth.

CLEAN WOODWORK.

Varnished woodwork and furniture that has become dull and cloudy can be clean and bright again. Just rub it with a soft cloth dipped in a solution of 1 tablespoon of white vinegar per quart of warm water. Buff with a soft, dry cloth to make the wood really shine.

CLEAN WOOD PANELING.

Here is a very good cleaning solution that leaves a nice finish on wood paneling and is also easy on the hands. It works much better and is much cheaper than any product you can buy. Mix 4 tablespoons of vinegar, 2 tablespoons of olive oil, and 1 pint of warm water. Apply with a cloth. No need to rinse off.

REPAIR SCRATCHES IN WOOD.

Wood scratches can easily be concealed with vinegar and iodine. Simply mix equal parts in a small container and use a small brush to paint over the scratch. For dark wood add more iodine; for lighter woods add more vinegar.

REMOVE STAINS ON WOOD.

To remove dark stains from wood floors or furniture, first clean the area with coarse steel wool dipped in mineral spirits. Next, scrub the stain with vinegar, allowing it to penetrate for several minutes. Repeat, if necessary, then rinse with water and wax.

REMOVE WAX BUILDUP.

To remove wax buildup on leather-top tables, use a solution of ¼ cup vinegar and ½ cup water.

REMOVE FURNITURE POLISH BUILDUP.

To remove furniture polish buildup on wood, mix ½ cup vinegar with ½ cup water. Dip a soft cloth in the solution and wring it out. Rub the area with the damp cloth and dry immediately with another soft cloth.

REMOVE WATER RINGS ON WOOD FURNITURE.
Combine vinegar and olive oil in equal parts to remove white rings left by wet drinking glasses. Apply with a clean soft cloth and work the vinegar mixture into the wood in the direction of the grain to erase water rings.

REMOVE WATER RINGS FROM LEATHER.
Water rings can be removed from leather furniture (or leather-top tables) by sponging the white ring with white vinegar.

CLEAN VINYL UPHOLSTERY.
Clean furniture with vinyl upholstery by dampening an old towel or washcloth with full-strength vinegar and rubbing down the upholstery. Rub the upholstery with a cloth dipped in water to remove the vinegar. To keep vinyl furniture from becoming hard and brittle, clean often this way.

POLISH LEATHER FURNITURE.
Bring 2 cups of linseed oil to a boil and boil for 1 minute; cool. Add 1 cup vinegar and stir well; apply with a clean, soft cloth. Or, mix equal parts of linseed oil and vinegar, shake well, and apply with a clean, soft cloth. This polish will also keep leather from cracking when used regularly.

CLEAN WOOD FLOORS.
Using a soft cloth, wipe floors with a solution of equal parts vinegar and water.

CLEAN PIANO KEYS.
Mix ½ cup vinegar to 2 cups water and clean keys with a soft, lint-free cloth dipped into the solution and wrung out until almost dry. Wipe dry and leave the keyboard open.

■ Vinegar on the Carpet ■

CLEAN UP PET OR PEOPLE "ACCIDENTS."

Sprinkle vinegar on soiled area, wait a few minutes, then sponge from the center out. Blot with a dry cloth. Repeat, if necessary. Alternatively, combine a small amount of liquid detergent and 3 tablespoons vinegar in 1 quart of warm water. Sponge on soiled area until clean, rinse with a cloth dampened with warm water, then blot with a dry cloth.

REMOVE PAINT FROM CARPET.

Get water-based paint out of a carpet by sponging with a solution of 1 tablespoon vinegar and 1 tablespoon liquid detergent in 1 quart of warm water.

REMOVE CARPET STAINS.

To remove light carpet stains mix 2 tablespoons salt with ½ cup vinegar. Rub this on carpet stains and let dry. When dry, vacuum. For heavy stains, add 2 tablespoons borax to the mixture and follow the same procedure. To clean dirt spots from the carpet, brush heavy traffic areas and spots with a mixture of 1 cup white vinegar per gallon of water. Blot dry. To clean tough ground-in dirt and spots on carpets, try 1 tablespoon vinegar with 1 tablespoon cornstarch. Work into the spot with a soft cloth and leave it for two days before vacuuming.

BRIGHTEN CARPET.

To bring out the color in a rug, dip a clean broom into a mixture of 1 cup white vinegar and 1 gallon of water, then brush the rug with the broom. No need to rinse.

KEEP CARPET MILDEW AWAY.

Spray white vinegar on the underside of carpet and area rugs to avoid mildew from wet spills.

CLEAN INDOOR/OUTDOOR CARPET.
Mix 1 gallon of warm water, 1 cup vinegar, and 1 tablespoon dish soap. Brush the mixture on the carpeting and blot dry with towels.

■ In the Kitchen ■

Vinegar works wonders in the kitchen. Try some of these handy tips.

COPPER CLEANER.
You don't have to pay big bucks for copper cleaner to keep your copper-bottom aluminum pans looking like new. Just combine equal parts of salt and flour and add enough vinegar to make a thick paste. Rub the paste into the copper using a soft cloth. Let it sit a few minutes, rinse, and watch it shine.

LIME DEPOSIT REMOVER.
To keep water from leaving a lime deposit at the bottom of a double boiler or steamer, add about 1 teaspoon of vinegar to the water each time you use it.

NONSTICK-PAN STAIN REMOVER.
Remove stains from nonstick cookware to prolong the life of your pots and pans. Rub the pans with a cloth dipped in vinegar to remove the white spotty film caused by minerals in the water.

POT-AND-PAN SCOURING MIX.
Mix equal amounts of flour and salt. Add vinegar to make a paste. Rub on pans with a sponge; rinse. Use this mixture for hard-to-remove stains. You can easily remove normal food stains by soaking pots and pans in full-strength vinegar for thirty minutes, then wash in hot soapy water and rinse.

PAN DEODORIZER.

Quickly get rid of strong odors such as fish or onions by rinsing still-hot pots and pans with vinegar.

CORNING WARE CLEANER.

To remove food stuck or burned on Corning Ware dishes, add 4 parts water to 1 part vinegar and bring to a gentle boil. When the water cools down, you should be able to gently scrub off the food.

ALUMINUM STAIN REMOVER.

Cooking acidic foods can cause dark stains inside aluminum pots and pans. You can remove these stains by boiling a solution of 1 tablespoon of white vinegar to each cup of water in a pot or pan. Fill the pan up to about 1 inch above the dark area.

BROILER PAN CLEANER.

Mix together 1 cup cider or white vinegar and 2 tablespoons sugar and pour over the broiler pan while it's still hot. After dinner the broiler pan will be a snap to wash as you do your other pans.

STAINLESS-STEEL POT AND FLATWARE CLEANER.

To clean and shine stainless-steel pots and flatware, rub with a soft vinegar-soaked cloth.

FOOD-STAIN REMOVER.

Soak food-stained pots and pans in full-strength white vinegar for thirty minutes. Then rinse in hot soapy water. Vinegar will even get the spaghetti stains off!

RUST-SPOT REMOVER.

You can remove rust spots from iron skillets or pans by filling the pan with ¼ vinegar and water. Boil the vinegar and water solution for thirty minutes on low heat. Pour out the water and wipe the rust away.

Burned food remover.

You don't have to spend hours soaking tough burned food off pots and pans. Instead boil ¼ cup of white vinegar with enough water to cover the stuck-on food. After five minutes, it will loosen the food so you can wash it clean.

Gas stove cleaner.

Wash the grates on a gas stove once a week with vinegar, and they won't be greasy.

Oven residue cleaner.

To remove oven cleaner residue left after cleaning your oven, spray the surfaces with a solution of equal parts vinegar and water, then wipe down with a damp sponge. This simple trick eliminates the smoking that occurs the first time you use the oven after cleaning.

Oven grease cleaner.

To prevent grease buildup in your oven, dip a rag or sponge in white vinegar and use it to wipe out the oven.

Stainless-steel spot remover.

To remove spots on your stainless steel kitchen appliances and sink, rub them with a cloth dipped in full-strength white vinegar. Buff the stainless steel to a shine with a dry cloth.

Microwave cleaner.

Clean your microwave and eliminate odors with vinegar. Simply boil in the microwave a solution of ¼ cup white vinegar mixed with 1 cup water in a small bowl for five minutes. The steam from the vinegar water will remove any odors and will soften baked-on splatters. After the vinegar water cools down, dip a sponge or rag into the water and use it to wipe off the inside surfaces of the microwave.

HOT PLATE CLEANER.

Use full strength white vinegar on a cloth or sponge to clean hot-plate surfaces. It works great for both the cooking surface and the rest of the hot plate.

DISHWASHING LIQUID.

You don't need to buy the most expensive type of detergent to wash dishes by hand. Add a few tablespoons of vinegar to the dishwater to help cut the grease and make dishes shine.

BOTTLE, JAR, AND VASE CLEANER.

Remove dirt or film residue on bottles, jars, and vases by filling them with vinegar and letting them stand for several minutes or longer, if needed, then shake or brush vigorously. To use in a dishwasher, place a cup of vinegar on the bottom rack, run the machine for three to five minutes; replace the vinegar with a fresh cup, then complete the dish washing cycle, adding dish-washer detergent as usual.

GLASS AND CHINA STAIN REMOVER.

Boil vinegar in glass coffeepots once a week, wash, and rinse. Mix equal parts vinegar and salt and use to scrub away stains on china tea cups.

FLOWER VASE CLEANER.

Clean the film residue off the inside of flower vases, decanters or other small neck bottles by pouring the container about one-fourth full of white vinegar and shake. If the stains are not removed with the first try, add about two tablespoons of raw white rice into the vinegar and shake again. The rice will help loosen the dirt without scratching the vase or bottle.

GLASS ENHANCER.

To cut the soapy film on your cloudy glassware, place a cup of white vinegar on the bottom rack of the dishwasher, run for five minutes, then run through the entire cycle. A cup of white vinegar added to the dishwasher once a month will also reduce buildup. (Some glasses get a cloudy look to them from rubbing against each other in the dishwasher. Make sure that your glasses do not rub against each other during the wash cycle.)

GLASSWARE BRIGHTENER.

Add ½ cup of vinegar to the rinse water when washing glasses or stemware by hand. It will keep the glasses from spotting and it kills germs.

CRYSTAL CLEANER.

When washing crystal glasses add 2 tablespoons of vinegar to the wash water with your regular liquid soap. After washing, rinse in 1 part vinegar to 3 parts warm water; let the glasses air dry and they will sparkle.

WATER SPOT REMOVER.

Add a half cup of vinegar to the final rinse cycle of the dishwasher to get rid of water spots and germs on glasses.

DISHWASHER CLEANER.

Run a cup of vinegar through the whole dishwasher cycle once a month to reduce soap buildup on the inside of the machine and the pipes. You can add the vinegar in a coffee cup or small bowl on the top shelf with a full load of dishes.

DISH SOAP BOOSTER.

Add three tablespoons of vinegar to your bottle of liquid dish-washing soap. Shake the bottle to mix the liquids. This tip is valu-able because it makes the soap mild on your hands and the soap last longer. The best part is it makes your dishes, counter tops, and cabinets shine, shine, shine!

FILM REMOVER.

To remove the white film that builds up on cut glassware, soak the glassware in a sink of warm water with 2 cups of vinegar for one hour. If the vinegar bath does not remove the white film, soak paper towels in full-strength vinegar and wrap around the glassware. Leave the paper towels on the glasses for one hour, then rinse with clean water.

JAR DEODORIZER.

You can save money by reusing jars (such as mayonnaise or spaghetti sauce jars) for food storage. To remove any odors from the jars, rinse them in vinegar after washing them with hot soapy water.

FAUCET BRIGHTENER.

To make your kitchen faucet shine, dampen a sponge or cloth with full-strength vinegar and wipe away the dull film. Polish it with a soft, damp cloth.

SOAP SCUM CLEANER.

Remove soap buildup or stains on chrome fixtures by cleaning them with a mixture of one teaspoon salt dissolved in two tablespoons of white vinegar. The salt will remove the tough grime without scratching the fixtures.

GARBAGE DISPOSAL DEODORIZER.

To keep your garbage disposal clean and fresh smelling make some vinegar ice cubes. Mix one cup of vinegar in enough water to fill an ice cube tray, freeze the mixture, then grind the cubes through the disposal. Rinse with cold water.

SPONGE RENEWER.

Instead of throwing away sponges when they start to smell, renew them with a vinegar and water bath. Soak the sponges overnight in a solution of 1 quart water and ¼ cup white vinegar. In the morning they will be clean and smell fresh.

DRAIN OPENER AND DEODORIZER.

To help prevent grease buildup and to keep your drains fresh smelling, pour a half of a box of baking soda down the sink. Add one-half cup of vinegar. Cover the drain tightly for fifteen minutes, then flush with cold water. To keep drains odor-free pour ½ cup vinegar down them once a week.

DRAIN BOARD CLEANER.

To get rid of water stains on the drain board, pour a cup of vinegar over the board and let it soak in the sink overnight. In the morning rub off the stains and rinse with water.

MARBLE COUNTERTOP CLEANER.

Use a solution of vinegar and water (half and half) to clean marble countertops. Spray the countertops with the vinegar water and rinse with clean water. Vinegar does a great job cleaning marble, but be careful to quickly remove the vinegar solution. The acid in vinegar can affect the appearance of marble if left on the marble for more than a few minutes. Always rinse with water quickly after cleaning.

WOOD BLOCK CLEANER.

Clean, deodorize, and disinfect wood cutting blocks once a week with baking soda and vinegar. First rub the cutting block with baking soda; then spray on full strength white vinegar. The vinegar and baking soda will bubble and clean. Let it sit for five minutes, then rinse with water. Wipe down your cutting block with full strength white vinegar after each use. The vinegar will clean and absorb odors.

NO-WAX FLOOR CLEANER.

Wash no-wax or linoleum floors with a mixture of vinegar and water (add one cup vinegar to a bucket of warm water) because a diluted mixture of vinegar and water will not strip the finish like so many other cleaners will. You'll also end up with a nice shine without wax.

LINOLEUM CLEANER.

For really tough stains on linoleum floors, apply undiluted vinegar directly on the stain. Let the vinegar soak for twenty minutes before rinsing with clean water. If this does not remove the stain, pour more undiluted vinegar on the stain and allow it to soak for thirty minutes, then pour baking soda on the vinegar and scrub with a sponge or brush. Rinse with clean water.

CERAMIC TILE CLEANER.

The best cleaner for ceramic tile floors or unwaxed linoleum is vinegar. Use about ½ cup white vinegar to ½ bucket of warm water. This solution works better than any store-bought floor cleaning product. It makes the floors sparkle and shine.

REFRIGERATOR CLEANER.

Vinegar is ideal for cleaning the refrigerator because it cleans, and prevents mildew from forming. Wipe the outside of the refrigerator with a vinegar and water solution (half and half is a good mixture), especially around the handle. Open the door and give the rubber gasket and drawer fronts a quick swipe. To prevent mildew from forming in your refrigerator, wipe the inside walls and bins with full-strength vinegar after you've finished cleaning.

TOP OF REFRIGERATOR CLEANER.

Grease and dirt residue that forms on the top of the refrigerator and the stove will easily come clean when you wipe the surface down with full strength white vinegar.

SMEAR AND FINGERPRINTS CLEANER.

Use a solution of half vinegar and half water to clean fingerprints and smears off refrigerators and other kitchen appliances. Use a soft cloth to apply the vinegar mixture and use another dry cloth to buff to a shine.

ICE CUBE TRAY CLEANER.

Soak plastic ice-cube trays in white vinegar for several hours to remove tough stains and odors. Rinse with clean water before using.

BLENDER AND FOOD PROCESSOR CLEANER.

Fill the container with ½ cup vinegar, ½ teaspoon liquid detergent, and warm water. Cover and turn on, then rinse and dry. You shouldn't have to scrub at all.

KNIFE SHARPENER.

When sharpening knives, dampen the whetstone with vinegar and you'll be able to get a sharp edge on the knife quickly.

CAN OPENER CLEANER.

Clean the blade (wheel) of your electric can opener with an old toothbrush dipped in vinegar. Hold the brush under the blade (wheel) and turn on the machine. All the gunk will come off easily without scrubbing.

PLASTIC STORAGE CONTAINER CLEANER.

To remove greasy stains from plastic food storage containers (such as Tupperware) soak the containers in hot soapy water with ¼ cup white vinegar added. Let them soak for several hours or overnight. After soaking, rinse with hot water and use a sponge to wipe away the stains.

THERMOS BOTTLE CLEANER.

To clean a thermos bottle, add ¼ cup vinegar and enough warm water to fill. For tough stains such as coffee, add a tablespoon of rice (which acts as a gentle abrasive) with the vinegar and water. Shake it up and rinse.

COFFEE MAKER CLEANER.

To eliminate unpleasant lime deposits that can build up and clog your coffee maker, once a month fill the coffee maker with 2 cups white vinegar and 1 cup water; then run through the brew cycle. Rinse out the machine and run two cycles of clean water through the coffeepot. You will be surprised how much better your morning coffee will taste! Pour the vinegar water used to clean the coffeepot on your rubber drain board to remove soap scum and lime deposits.

TEAKETTLE CLEANER.
Remove lime and other deposits from a teakettle or teapot by filling it with equal parts of water and white vinegar. Bring the vinegar and water to a boil and let stand overnight. In the morning rinse with water.

GREASE REMOVER.
Keep a bottle of vinegar within easy reach. When your stove, counter tops, walls, or anything else becomes spattered with grease, dip a sponge in full-strength vinegar and wipe the greasy surface. Rinse with clean water and dry with a soft cloth. Vinegar cuts the grease and leaves a nice shine.

CHROME FURNITURE CLEANER.
Clean and polish chrome table and chair legs with vinegar. Simply rub the legs with a cloth moistened with white vinegar.

LUNCH BOX DEODORIZER.
To get rid of odors, dampen a piece of bread with white vinegar and place it in the lunch box overnight. In the morning, wash the lunch box with hot soapy water, and it will be clean and fresh smelling.

KITCHEN DEODORIZER.
For an inexpensive deodorizer place a small cup half full of vinegar in the kitchen. You can use this anytime, and it will absorb even strong odors like cabbage for just pennies! Once a week replace the vinegar to keep the kitchen smelling fresh. Pour the used vinegar down the disposal to keep it from clogging.

BREAD BOX FRESHENER.

After cleaning your bread box, keep it smelling fresh by wiping the inside with a sponge or cloth dampened with white vinegar.

COOKING ODOR REMOVER.

Prevent the odor of boiling cabbage by adding a little vinegar to the cooking water. Pour vinegar into the hot skillet or pan after cooking fish or onions and let it simmer for a few minutes. Boil 1 tablespoon of vinegar in 1 cup of water for five minutes to eliminate cooking odors from the room.

BERRY STAIN REMOVER.

Rub hands with vinegar to remove fruit stains.

ONION ODOR ELIMINATOR.

Rub vinegar on your hands before and after cutting onions and your hands won't have a lingering onion smell.

■ In the Home Office ■

CLEAN OFFICE EQUIPMENT.

Many of us now have computers, printers, fax machines, and other types of office equipment at home. You can clean them all with a vinegar-and-water solution. Mix half vinegar and half water. Dip a cloth or sponge into the mixture and wring out as much moisture as possible. After first turning them off, wipe down the outside of your computer, printer, and other pieces of equipment with the vinegar solution. Never use a spray bottle for this job. You want to make sure that moisture does not get inside the equipment. For delicate areas such as the keyboard, use a cotton swab dipped in the vinegar mixture. Wring it out to remove any excess moisture. Wipe equipment clean often to keep dust and dirt from accumulating.

CLEAN YOUR COMPUTER MOUSE.

When your computer mouse gets dirty and picks up dust, it becomes hard to manipulate. If you can easily remove the ball inside your mouse, you can clean it with a vinegar solution instead of buying a special cleaner. Mix half vinegar and half water. Be sure the computer is off! Remove the ball and wipe clean with the vinegar solution. Dry thoroughly with a soft, lint-free towel. Dip a cotton swab into the vinegar mixture and wipe inside the mouse, removing dust or dirt particles. Dry thoroughly. Dip a soft cloth into the vinegar mixture and wring out as much moisture as possible. Use this cloth to wipe clean the outside of the mouse and the cord.

CLEAN SCISSORS.

When you find that your scissors have become sticky (from cutting tape or a tacky surface), clean them with a rag dipped in full-strength white vinegar.

THIN GLUE.

Instead of throwing away glue that has thickened in the bottle, insert a drop or two of vinegar and shake. Keep adding vinegar drop by drop until the glue returns to the proper consistency.

■ In the Bathroom ■

Vinegar can be used to clean almost everything in the bathroom. It also disinfects and makes your bathroom sparkle. As with all other cleaning projects, this one requires the use of either white distilled vinegar or inexpensive apple cider vinegar.

CLEAN THE SHOWER STALL.

Remove dirt, grime, soap buildup, and hard-water stains by wiping them with a sponge dampened with vinegar. Rinse with clean water.

REMOVE SHOWER DOOR SPOTS.

Dip a sponge in a vinegar-and-water solution (2 cups vinegar and 1 gallon water) and use it to remove water spots on glass shower doors. For tough stains use full-strength vinegar. Rinse with clean water.

CLEAN SHOWER DOOR TRACKS.

Shower door tracks will come clean easily if you fill the tracks with vinegar and leave it for several hours. Pour hot water in the tracks to wash away the built-up dirt. Use a brush to scrub away any tough spots. For especially dirty tracks heat the vinegar in the microwave or in a glass pan or plastic container before pouring it into the tracks. This will help loosen the stuck-on gunk.

CLEAN SHOWER CURTAINS.

Use full-strength vinegar on a shower curtain to wipe away soapy film, mildew, or dirt buildup. The easiest way to get a plastic shower curtain really clean is to wash it in the washing machine. Fill the washing machine with warm water and two or three dirty towels (we all have plenty). Add ½ cup laundry detergent and ½ cup baking soda. Then wash on regular cycle, adding 1 cup white vinegar to the rinse. (If your shower curtain is delicate, use the gentle cycle.) Pull the shower curtain out after the rinse cycle, then let the towels continue through the spin dry cycle. Hang the shower curtain back up immediately, and the wrinkles will disappear as the curtain dries. This is easy, so you won't be tempted to throw it away when it gets dirty.

CLEANING REMOVABLE SHOWERHEADS.

To unclog a metal showerhead, bring ½ cup vinegar and 1 quart of water to a boil. Then place the showerhead in the boiling solution for ten minutes. If you have a plastic showerhead, soak it in equal amounts of hot (not boiling) vinegar and water.

CLEANING NONREMOVABLE SHOWERHEADS.

To clean that nasty scum off nonremovable showerheads, take a little plastic bag and fill it halfway with vinegar. Tape it on the showerhead so that the showerhead is immersed in the vinegar. Wait ½ hour to 1 hour depending on how bad the buildup is. Remove the bag, wipe off the vinegar, and the showerhead should be as clean as new.

CLEAN HARD-WATER SPOTS.

If you have hard-water or lime spots on the tub or sink, cover them with vinegar-soaked paper towels. Let the vinegar soak for an hour or so, remove the towels, and then scrub with a dampened plastic scrubber sprinkled with a little baking soda. Repeat if necessary.

CLEAN SINKS AND TUBS.

Clean the bathtub and sinks with full-strength vinegar. Simply scrub the surface with vinegar and rinse with water. Your tub and sinks will shine!

SHINE FAUCETS.

To make your bathroom faucets shine, dampen a sponge or cloth with vinegar and wipe away the dull film. Polish them with a soft, damp cloth.

CLEAN FIXTURES.

To clean the stubborn dirt and grime that accumulates at the base of bathroom fixtures, wrap toilet paper around the base of the sink or toilet, saturate with vinegar; let it sit for about thirty minutes. Remove the paper and brush away the grime with an old toothbrush.

BATH DECAL REMOVAL.

To remove really stubborn bathtub decals, use full-strength vinegar. Pour the vinegar around the edges of the decal and let it soak for thirty minutes. This should loosen them so you can pull them off. Use a little more vinegar to clean off any stubborn sticky residue. Rinse away the vinegar with soapy water.

CLEAN TILE GROUT.

Dip an old toothbrush in full strength vinegar and use it to scrub away the dirt on tile grout. It will remove tough stains without harming the grout.

CLEAN CERAMIC TILES.

To clean ceramic tiles, wash them with a solution of ½ cup white vinegar, ½ cup ammonia, ¼ cup borax, and 1 gallon of warm water. Rinse with clean water and let dry.

PREVENT MOLD AND MILDEW.

To prevent mold and mildew in a humid bathroom, mix 1 teaspoon borax, 3 tablespoons vinegar, and 2 cups hot water. Put in a spray bottle and shake to mix. Spray on tile, tub, and other mold-prone areas. Don't rinse—the solution will evaporate.

CLEAN TOILET BOWLS.

Cleaning the toilet bowl is quick and easy when you use vinegar. Simply pour 2 cups white vinegar in the bowl and let it soak overnight. Flush the next morning. If the toilet bowl ring is particularly tough, you may have to scrub the first time to remove it; but if you clean the bowl frequently with vinegar, you won't even have to scrub!

REMOVE RUST AND LIME DEPOSITS FROM TOILET.

To clean rust or lime deposits on the toilet bowl above the water line, drape the bowl with several thicknesses of paper towels that cover the rust line and then pour vinegar on the towels to saturate them. Keep the paper towels moist with vinegar until the lime deposits dissolve.

CLEAN AND DEODORIZE DRAINS.

Clean soap scum and water residue from tub and sink drains with ½ cup baking soda and 1 cup vinegar. This will also take away any bad odors in the drains. Just pour the baking soda down the drain and follow it with the vinegar, let it sit for a few minutes, and flush with water. Do this often (twice a month) to keep drains from clogging.

OPEN DRAINS.

You can open a stopped-up sink drain by pouring ¼ cup baking soda down the drain, then adding ½ cup white vinegar. Cover the drain for a few minutes, then flush with cold water.

SOFTEN A STIFF TOOTHBRUSH.

Soak a stiff toothbrush in hot vinegar for 30 minutes; then rinse with water.

■ Vinegar in the Laundry ■

In the laundry room vinegar can work wonders. White distilled vinegar is the best in the following applications, since apple cider vinegar may stain clothing a brownish color.

NEW CLOTHES TREATMENT.

Add one cup vinegar to the wash cycle when cleaning new clothes in the washing machine. It will help eliminate manufacturing chemicals and their odors.

LAUNDRY BRIGHTENER.

Instead of buying an expensive all-color bleach product, add ½ cup of white vinegar to each load. Vinegar will help clean and brighten colorful clothes.

COLOR CORRECTOR.

Bright colored clothes have a tendency to run, but if you immerse them in full-strength white vinegar before washing, your garments will remain true to their colors.

FABRIC DYE SETTER.

After dyeing fabric, set the color by adding 1 cup of vinegar to the last rinse water.

CLOTHES WHITENER.
Add 1½ cups vinegar to rinse water to brighten white laundry.

SOCK WHITENER.
Restore dingy (or gray) white socks to a bright white color by soaking them in vinegar and hot water. Fill a large pot half full with tap water and add 1 cup vinegar. Bring the water to a boil and remove from the stove. Place socks in the hot water and let them soak overnight or until the water is cool. Wash as usual.

PERSPIRATION ODOR ELIMINATOR.
Perspiration odor and stains can be removed from clothes with vinegar. Pour some full-strength vinegar on the underarm area and the collar before washing.

SMOKE ODOR REMOVER.
After a party your clothes may be full of cigarette smoke. Pour 2 cups of vinegar in a bathtub of hot water, hang the clothes above the tub, and let the clothes hang for several hours to remove the odors. This is especially helpful for coats and jackets that are too expensive to dry-clean after each party.

SKUNK ODOR REMOVER.
To remove skunk odor from clothing, soak the items in a solution of 1 cup vinegar in 1 gallon of water. Leave the clothes in the vinegar bath for several hours or overnight to remove the smell.

SUDS REDUCER.
Get rid of excess suds in either hand or machine washes by adding a cup of vinegar to the rinse water, followed by a clear-water rinse.

HEAVY-DUTY CLEANER.
Soak heavily soiled items in a bucket of warm water with 1 cup of vinegar. Wash as usual.

FABRIC SOFTENER.

Vinegar can be used to make all your clothes soft. Add one cup of vinegar to each wash load during the rinse cycle. This works great for baby clothes or any family members that may be sensitive to fabric softeners. When added to the last rinse, vinegar also eliminates static electricity.

LINT ELIMINATOR.

To keep lint from clinging to clothing, especially dark garments, add ½ cup vinegar to the last rinse cycle.

CORDUROY CONDITIONER.

When washing corduroy garments, add ½ cup vinegar to the rinse water. The fabric will be lint-free and the color brighter.

BLANKET AND SWEATER SOFTENER.

Add 2 cups of vinegar to rinse water to remove soap odor and make material soft and fluffy.

DRAPES SOFTENER.

Add ¼ cup vinegar to the rinse cycle when laundering drapes or synthetic curtains to soften and reduce static and wrinkles.

SHOWER CURTAIN CLEANER.

To remove mildew and soap scum from plastic or cloth shower curtains, launder the curtain with several bath towels in the washing machine. Add one cup of vinegar during the rinse cycle. Remove from the washing machine and hang to dry. The vinegar also helps eliminate wrinkles.

SILK RINSE.

After hand-washing silk clothing in mild soap, remove soap residue by adding a tablespoon of vinegar to clean, cool rinse water. Roll the clothing article in a towel to remove excess water; hang or lay it flat until slightly damp. Press on wrong side with a cool iron.

PANTY HOSE AND LINGERIE PRESERVER.
Add 1 teaspoon vinegar to the rinse water. This will help panty hose and lingerie retain their elasticity.

CHEWING GUM REMOVER.
Vinegar removes gum from fabric, carpet, and upholstery. Pour a little full-strength vinegar on the gum and let it sit for ten to fifteen minutes. The vinegar will help loosen the gum from the fabric.

WINE AND KETCHUP STAIN REMOVER.
Sponge washable cotton polyester and blends with vinegar within twenty-four hours. Launder as usual as soon as possible.

NONOILY STAIN REMOVER.
Remove nonoily, water-soluble stains such as wine, perspiration, fruit juice, alcoholic drinks, coffee, tea, soft drinks, salt water, or vomit from fabric by one of these two methods: (1) for washable clothing, either dab the area with a clean soft cloth dampened in vinegar and immediately wash as usual or (2) soak the garment in a mixture of 3 parts vinegar to 1 part cool water for several hours or overnight before washing as usual.

CRAYON STAIN REMOVER.
Moisten an old soft toothbrush with vinegar and rub crayon stains out of clothing. Wash as usual.

HAIR-DYE STAIN REMOVER.
Apply some full-strength vinegar to the stain before washing. To remove stubborn hair-dye stains from clothing, add 2 cups vinegar to the wash cycle. For the best success, treat hair-dye stains as soon as possible.

MILDEW REMOVER.
To remove mildew from washable fabrics, soak them in sour milk. If you don't have any sour milk, you can make some by

adding 1 teaspoon vinegar to 1 cup of milk. Pour the sour milk on the mildew spots and let dry in the sun. Wash as usual, and the mildew should disappear.

DEODORANT STAIN REMOVER.
To remove stains left on clothing from deodorant and antiperspirant, rub the fabric lightly with vinegar. Launder as usual.

INK STAIN REMOVER.
Remove ink marks from fabric by moistening the area with vinegar, then applying a paste of vinegar and cornstarch. Let the paste dry before washing the garment as usual.

BARBECUE-SAUCE STAIN REMOVER.
Sponge stains with a solution of equal amounts of vinegar and water. Wash in warm water. Don't use hot water or place the garment into the dryer until the stain is removed because heat will set the stain.

RUST STAIN REMOVER.
Moisten washable fabric with vinegar, then rub in some salt. Place in the sun to dry, then launder as usual.

RING-AROUND-THE-COLLAR REMOVER.
Use a vinegar-and-baking-soda paste as a prewash treatment for dirty cuffs, collars, and mildew stains on clothing. Scrub the stains with a paste of three parts baking soda and two parts white vinegar. Leave the paste on the collar for thirty minutes. Launder as usual.

BALLPOINT PEN MARK REMOVER.
A fresh ballpoint pen mark can often be removed with a little hair spray. Spray on the spot and let dry. Then brush lightly with a solution of half water and half vinegar.

SET-IN STAIN REMOVER.

To remove older stains on clothes, combine 2 tablespoons of liquid detergent, 3 tablespoons of vinegar, and 1 quart of warm water. Work into the stain and blot dry. Wash as usual.

WINE AND COLA STAIN REMOVER.

Vinegar will remove wine or cola stains with ease if you apply it to the stain within twenty-four hours. Apply white vinegar directly to the stain (on washable fabrics only). Wash immediately as usual.

LINEN PRESERVER.

One cup of vinegar in the rinse water of linens, such as tablecloths, napkins, sheets, and pillowcases, keeps them from yellowing in storage.

YELLOWED CLOTHES REVIVER.

Yellowed clothes can be revived by soaking them in a solution of 12 parts water to 1 part white vinegar. Leave the yellowed clothes in the mixture overnight and wash as usual the next day.

SHRUNKEN SWEATER SAVER.

Boil a shrunken wool garment in 1 part vinegar and 2 parts water for twenty-five minutes. Reshape the garment and allow to air-dry.

WASHING MACHINE CLEANER.

Add 2 cups of vinegar to the washing machine when washing especially dirty clothes. The vinegar not only will help clean the clothes but will also dissolve soap scum in the washing machine hoses.

WRINKLE REMOVER.

To get wrinkles out of clothing that has been washed and dried, spray with a mixture of 1 part white vinegar and 3 parts water.

Mist evenly, shake the clothing, and hang to dry. The wrinkles come out immediately, and the vinegar smell disappears in about ten minutes. This method will make your clothes last longer because it is easier on the fabric than ironing. This is particularly helpful for golf shirts.

FABRIC-CREASE AND THREAD-HOLE REMOVER.
When lengthening a hem, changing a crease, or opening a seam, make a solution of equal parts vinegar and water, then use it to dampen a pressing cloth. Iron as usual, and the thread holes will magically disappear.

CREASE SHARPENER.
Dampen fabric with a cloth moistened in a solution of 1 part vinegar to 2 parts water. Place heavy brown paper over the crease and press.

ELECTRIC IRON CLEANER.
To remove dark or burned spots on the bottom of an iron, rub with a mixture of half vinegar and half salt, then wipe off with a rag dipped in clean water.

STARCH BUILDUP REMOVER.
To remove starch buildup from an iron, simply wipe it clean with a moist cloth dipped in full-strength white vinegar. Note: For safety reasons, always clean the iron while it is unplugged and cold.

STEAM-IRON CLEANER.
To clean the inside of a steam iron, occasionally fill the water reservoir with full-strength white vinegar and let the vinegar steam-clean the iron. Repeat the process using water, then thoroughly rinse out the inside of the iron with clean water. This will keep your iron free of corrosion and of calcium or lime deposits.

SCORCH MARK REMOVER.

With a soft, clean cloth dampened in vinegar, lightly rub scorched fabric. Wipe with a clean, dry cloth. This method is effective for light scorch marks but not for heavily scorched items.

SHINE PREVENTER.

To keep wool and other fabrics from becoming shiny when ironing, place a thin cloth dampened with 1 part vinegar to 2 parts water over the fabric.

CLOTHES HAMPER CLEANER.

When you empty out the clothes hamper to do the wash, wipe down the inside with full-strength vinegar to eliminate odors. Sprinkle some baking soda in the bottom, and it will stay fresh smelling.

WINTER CLOTHESLINE HELPER.

Wet clothes won't freeze onto the clothesline if you first wipe the line with a cloth dampened in full-strength vinegar.

SUEDE CLEANER.

To clean and condition suede garments, wipe them with a sponge or soft cloth dipped in vinegar. To remove grease stains from suede, rub gently with a cloth dipped in vinegar. Brush with a suede brush when dry.

SPOT REMOVER FOR SUEDE SHOES.

To get rid of those shiny spots on suede shoes, put a drop of vinegar on the area and allow it to dry. Use a suede brush to remove the spots.

SALT REMOVER FOR BOOTS AND SHOES.

Rescue shoes or boots from the damaging effects of salt by cleaning with vinegar. To remove salt, pour undiluted white vinegar on a damp cloth and wipe on the affected areas. Polish with a soft cloth.

Patent leather shoe shiner.

To clean and shine patent leather shoes quickly and easily, dip a sponge in vinegar and wipe the shoes clean. Buff to a high shine with a soft, dry cloth.

Shoe polish helper.

After you've put polish on your shoes, buff with a few drops of vinegar. They'll shine like new.

■ Vinegar in the Workroom ■

Protect drill bits.

Use vinegar as a cutting agent for drilling holes in metal. Simply pour some vinegar over the drill bit before using. It really extends the life of drill bits.

Loosen rusted, corroded screws and hinges.

Pour vinegar over the head of a rusty screw or hinge to loosen it. Clean rusty screws, bolts, and nuts by soaking them in vinegar and scrubbing them with a brush, if necessary.

Remove rust.

Use white or apple cider vinegar to remove rust from old tools you may have on hand or ones purchased at yard sales. Vinegar will also loosen any moving part on a tool that may have stiffened.

Prime metal.

Prime galvanized metal before painting by scouring it with vinegar. Let the metal dry completely before painting. The paint will go on easily, and you won't have to touch it up as often.

Clean and soften paint brushes.

Soak mildly caked paint brushes in vinegar until clean and soft. To clean hardened paint brushes that seem destined for the trash can, simmer them in boiling vinegar for a few minutes before washing in warm, soapy water.

REMOVE DRIED PAINT ON GLASS.

Apply heated vinegar to splattered paint on a glass window, then scrape off the now softened paint with an expired credit card or a razor blade.

ELIMINATE PAINT FUMES.

Keep a dish or two of vinegar in the room while painting. The vinegar will absorb the strong paint fumes. An old-time remedy for eliminating paint fumes is to take a bucket and fill it half full with hay. Sprinkle 1 cup vinegar over the hay. Let this sit for twenty minutes, then add enough water to cover the hay. This is handy for a painting project that might take longer than a day to complete. If you don't happen to have any hay, you can use old shredded newspapers instead.

RETARD PLASTER.

Slow the hardening of plaster by adding a little white vinegar to the mixture. It will still harden properly; you just get a little more time to work with it.

LOOSEN OLD GLUE IN FURNITURE JOINTS.

When disassembling furniture legs, shelves, and joints to reglue, fill a squirt bottle with vinegar and apply to the joint. For tough jobs, heat the vinegar before using. The warm vinegar will penetrate quickly.

CATCH SAWDUST.

While wiping up dust or sawdust, add some vinegar to the water to speed up the process. This is helpful when cleaning up after a big home-improvement project.

REMOVE WALLPAPER.

Dip a sponge into hot vinegar water (mix half water and half vinegar) and rub over wallpaper you want to remove. Before you know it, the wallpaper will peel right off. If the wallpaper is especially old, heat the vinegar water almost to the boiling point and apply the very hot vinegar water to the wallpaper and let it soak in until the paper starts to peel. After you get a corner started, pour some hot vinegar water on the wall so it can get underneath the old wallpaper and speed up the process.

REMOVE CEMENT FROM HANDS.

To clean hands after working in cement or concrete, wash them in full-strength vinegar, then rinse in water.

■ Vinegar in the Car ■

REMOVE BUMPER STICKERS.

Apply full-strength vinegar directly on top and around the edges to remove old bumper stickers. Give the vinegar time to soak in and then gently scrape off. An old credit card is perfect for scrapping off the old sticker or decal. Use more vinegar if the sticky mess remains. Use the same procedure to remove the price sticker from the window of a new car.

CLEAN CAR CHROME.

Few new cars contain chrome, but if you have a vintage baby, clean the chrome with vinegar, and it will sparkle like new. Pour a little full-strength vinegar on a rag and buff to a high shine.

CLEAN CAR CARPETING.

Use a mixture of half water and half white vinegar to remove dirt and stains from car carpeting. Simply sponge the vinegar/water mixture on the carpet and blot up with a towel. This formula will also remove the salt residue left on carpets after the winter snow season.

CLEAN PLASTIC UPHOLSTERY.
Wipe plastic or vinyl upholstery with a soft cloth dampened with a solution of half water and half vinegar.

DEFROST CAR WINDOWS.
During the winter if you have to leave your car outside, coat the outside of the car windows with a solution of 3 parts white or cider vinegar to 1 part water. This will keep the windows frost-free for several months.

CLEAN WINDSHIELDS.
Keep a small spray bottle full of white vinegar and some paper towels, rags, or even old newspapers inside your car to clean the grease and grime off the windshield. Vinegar will also remove any hazy film that builds up on the windows.

■ Vinegar in the Garden and Outside ■

REMEDY YELLOW LEAF.
Gardenias, azaleas, rhododendrons, and other plants that need an acidic soil develop yellow leaves as a result of excess lime in hard water, which prevents them from taking enough iron from the soil. To remedy the solution, mix 2 tablespoons cider vinegar to a quart of water and pour 1 cup of the mixture on the dirt around the plant every three weeks to make the leaves green again.

KILL GARDEN BUGS.
To eliminate bugs that are eating your fruits and vegetables, mix 1 cup sugar and 1 cup vinegar together. Cut a banana peel into small pieces and mix with the sugar and vinegar. Pour the bug killer into a plastic milk jug and hang it in a tree or place it in the garden to attract the bugs.

TREAT GARDEN MILDEW AND FUNGUS.

Look no further than your kitchen pantry to make this effective, organic formula.

Fill a 1-gallon sprayer half full with water. Add 1½ tablespoons baking soda, 1 tablespoon white vinegar, and 1 teaspoon vegetable oil. Fill to the top with water and shake well. Spray tops and undersides of leaves and stems of plants. Repeat every three to four days until disease is under control. Repeat after a rain, since the rain will wash away the formula.

KILL WEEDS.

To kill weeds and grass growing in sidewalk or driveway cracks, just pour full-strength vinegar on them. Vinegar is a natural alternative to harsh lawn chemicals.

KILL DANDELIONS.

You can keep your yard dandelion-free with vinegar. Fill a spray bottle with undiluted vinegar. When dandelions start to pop up, spray the center of each flower with the vinegar. Spray once directly on the plant and again near the ground so the vinegar can soak into the roots. This will kill the dandelions and keep them from growing back. It is best to do this on a sunny day when no rain is expected for a few days, because the rain will wash away the vinegar.

EXTEND LIFE OF CUT FLOWERS.

Cut flowers will stay fresh longer if vinegar is added to their water. Combine 2 tablespoons vinegar, 3 tablespoons sugar, and a quart of warm water. Add the mixture to the vase as needed. Stems should be in 3 to 4 inches of water for best results.

WASH HOUSEPLANTS.

Keep houseplants looking great by cleaning and shining the leaves with a vinegar-and-water solution. Simply wipe them gently with a soft cloth that has been dipped into a solution of ½ cup white vinegar and a gallon of cool tap water.

START SEEDS.

To improve germination of woody-coated seeds (asparagus, cardinal climber, cypress vine, morning glory, okra, and sweet peas), rub seeds between two sheets of coarse sandpaper, then soak overnight in a pint of warm water with ½ cup vinegar and a squirt of liquid soap. Plant the seeds the next day. Use water treatment without sandpaper for nasturtium, parsley, parsnip, and beet seeds.

CLEAN CLAY POTS.

Wash away dirt and white rings from clay pots by using a solution of half vinegar and half water.

CLEAN WOOD PATIO FURNITURE.

To remove dirt and mildew from wood patio furniture, mix together 1 cup ammonia, ½ cup white vinegar, ¼ cup baking soda, and 1 gallon water. Use a sponge or brush to apply the mixture and to scrub the tough stains.

CLEAN PLASTIC OR MESH PATIO FURNITURE.

To clean, deodorize, and stop the growth of mildew on plastic or mesh patio furniture, clean it with a mixture of hot soapy water and vinegar. Start with a bucket of hot water; add 2 tablespoons liquid soap and 2 cups white vinegar. Use a soft brush to work the mixture into the padding of the furniture. Rinse with clean water and let dry in the sun. Use the same formula to clean patio umbrellas.

REMOVE CONCRETE RUST STAINS.

Rust stains from metal patio furniture can be removed from concrete by pouring on full-strength white vinegar and allowing it to soak for a few minutes before wiping it off with a cloth. The older the stain, the longer you will need to let the vinegar soak before wiping it up.

DEODORIZE ICE CHESTS.

After ice chests (coolers) have been stored for the long winter, they tend to have a musty or stale odor. First clean the ice chest with hot soapy water. Then leave a small bowl full of vinegar inside the closed ice chest overnight. In the morning it will be clean and fresh smelling.

KEEP HIKING OR CAMPING WATER FRESH.

Add several drops of vinegar to the water in a canteen or thermos of water to keep it fresh longer and make it a better thirst quencher.

EXTEND LIFE OF PROPANE LANTERNS.

For longer-lasting and brighter-burning propane lanterns, soak the new wicks for several hours in full-strength white vinegar and let them dry before inserting. Your flame will be much brighter without using extra fuel.

CONDITION HANDS FOR COLD WEATHER.

Rinse your hands in vinegar and dry them thoroughly before going outside to work in very cold weather. The vinegar conditions your hands so that your fingers remain limber a little longer.

■ Vinegar for Pets, Country Animals, and Pests ■

DEODORIZE CAT LITTER BOX.

To remove cat-box odor, wash the litter box with sudsy water and rinse. Then mix 1 cup white vinegar into a gallon of water. Pour the vinegar-and-water mixture into the litter box and let it soak five minutes or longer, then rinse thoroughly with clean water.

CLEAN UP A PUPPY (OR OTHER ANIMAL) ACCIDENT.

Blot up as much urine from the carpet as possible, then rub the spot with a mixture of half white vinegar and the same amount of warm, sudsy water. Blot thoroughly, then pour some more vinegar and water over the spot. Place a dry towel over the area with a heavy book on top. Once the towel is soggy, replace it with a clean, dry one. The spot will be clean and deodorized.

CONTROL FLEAS AND TICKS.
To help keep a pet free of fleas and ticks, add 1 teaspoon of vinegar to each quart of the animal's drinking water.

IMPROVE PET HEALTH.
To improve a dog's or cat's health, add 1 teaspoon of vinegar to his fresh water each day to provide nutrients not found in pet food.

CLEAN OUT PET'S EARS.
Use a soft cloth or a cotton swab dipped in vinegar diluted with a little water to clean inside your dog's ears. The vinegar will help keep his ears clean and dry, so he will not scratch them as much. The vinegar cleans and controls yeast and bacteria.

REDUCE SOAP FILM.
When bathing a cat or dog, cut down on the soap film and eliminate the strong soap odor by adding vinegar to the rinse water. This will also make a pet's hair soft.

BATHE WITH A SPONGE.
Instead of giving your short-haired pet a full bath, sponge him clean with vinegar water. Mix together ½ cup vinegar in 1 quart water. Dip a sponge or cloth into the water and rub your pet clean. This quick and easy method will also eliminate odors.

CLEAN FISH BOWLS.
That white deposit in the goldfish bowl can quickly be removed by rubbing it with a cloth dipped in white vinegar. Rinse well.

ALLEVIATE PET ARTHRITIS.
Vinegar is good for pets with arthritis. Pour white vinegar on a soft cloth and use the cloth to soak the joints. Wrap the vinegar-

soaked cloth around the joints and leave it on for ten minutes at a time. Repeat the process twice a day.

CLEAN PET BOWLS.
When your pet's water dish gets coated with lime, soak it in vinegar and water until the lime is loosened and rinses out.

PORCUPINE QUILL REMEDY.
To remove porcupine quills from pets, mix 2 teaspoons of baking soda with 1 cup vinegar and pat on the quills. Wait ten minutes, reapply, wait another ten minutes, and remove the quills.

SKUNK SMELL.
If your pet should get sprayed by a skunk, combine equal parts of vinegar and water. Bathe the pet thoroughly in the solution and rinse with water. Repeat but use less vinegar.

PECKING CHICKENS.
To keep chicks from pecking at each other, put vinegar in their water every day. Add ¼ cup vinegar per gallon of fresh water.

INCREASED CHICKEN GROWTH.
When apple cider vinegar is added to the drinking water of chickens, they will feather out faster, grow tail feathers quicker, and gain weight faster.

MORE MILK.
When vinegar is added to a dairy cow's food, she will produce more milk.

TENDER BEEF.
The potassium in vinegar will make the meat of a dairy cow or bull tender when it is sent to market for beef. Simply add 2 tablespoons of vinegar to the food or water twice daily.

NEW COW.
Dairy farmers report that a new cow is quickly accepted into the herd when she is sprayed with a solution of vinegar and water.

TRASH SOLUTION.
When you put out the trash, spray a little vinegar on the bags or trash cans. It will keep dogs, cats, and other stray animals from scattering your trash all over the neighborhood.

ANT ABOLISHER.
Instead of using harsh and expensive insecticides to keep ants away, use vinegar. Spread a solution of half vinegar and half water all around the areas where ants can enter the house. Use a sponge to wipe down doorjams, windowsills, and foundation cracks. Be careful not to pour this mixture on plants or shrubs!

ANT KILLER.
For outdoor killing of small ants that travel in a single file, a spray of white vinegar kills them instantly, right before your eyes. It really works! Use an empty small plastic bottle. This is especially useful if you don't have any ant killer on hand, since you probably always have vinegar on the shelf.

GARDEN PROTECTOR.
Soak pieces of paper in vinegar and put them around the edges of the garden. This will keep cats, dogs, rabbits, and other animals away from your garden. Replace the vinegar-soaked paper once a week.

GNAT DEFENSE.
To keep the gnats and mosquitoes away while you're outside, rub a little cider vinegar on all exposed skin.

■ Vinegar Tips for Parents ■

Vinegar is the best cleaning choice for many chores dealing with children. Because it does not contain the harmful chemicals found in many commercial cleaning products, you can feel good about using it around little ones.

CLEAN BABY BOTTLES.
Soak bottles in vinegar for several hours to remove stains and hard-water film. Rinse thoroughly.

PRESOAK DIAPERS.
Rinse cloth diapers in the toilet or tub and soak them in a solution of 1 part vinegar and 10 parts water. Wash as usual.

CLEAN DIAPER PAIL.
After removing dirty diapers, wash the diaper pail with hot soapy water, then rub the inside with full-strength vinegar. It will eliminate the odors (at least for a while!).

WASH BABY CLOTHES AND DIAPERS.
Add a cup of vinegar to the rinse cycle to break down uric acid and soap residue. The vinegar will leave baby clothes soft and less likely to cause a rash.

CLEAN AND DISINFECT THE HIGHCHAIR.
Spray or wipe the highchair clean with a vinegar-and-water solution (combine half vinegar and half water). It will remove food particles and disinfect it too.

CLEAN AND DISINFECT BABY TOYS.
Add 1 cup of vinegar and 1 tablespoon of liquid soap to a sink of hot water to disinfect baby toys. Be careful to rinse well after cleaning.

CLEAN PLASTIC DOLLS.

Wash plastic dolls with full-strength vinegar to remove dirt. Clean the doll clothes by soaking them in a quart of warm water with 2 tablespoons of baking soda and 3 tablespoons of vinegar. Rinse with water and let air dry.

CLEAN THE SWING SET.

The plastic or wood seats of children's swing sets get very dirty from being outside all the time. Clean often with a solution of half white vinegar and half water. For hard-to-remove stains, let the solution soak for a few minutes before sprinkling with baking soda. Then scrub with a rag or brush to remove the tough stains. Rinse with clean water.

CLEAN OUTSIDE TOYS.

Use the same method as described above for swing sets to clean children's such toys as plastic three-wheeled cycles and pedal cars.

CLEAN BOOK COVERS.

Wipe a cloth dampened in a solution of 1 part vinegar and 2 parts water to clean the outside of your children's favorite cloth, vinyl, and board books. Do not use on thin paper.

CLEAN SPORTS EQUIPMENT.

To remove mud and dirt stains from plastic, fiberglass, and aluminum equipment, apply a paste of 1 part vinegar and 3 parts baking soda. Wipe off the paste with soapy water and rinse with clean water.

REMOVE CRAYON STAINS.

Moisten a soft toothbrush with vinegar to gently brush away crayon stains on fabrics, walls, and other surfaces.

DYE EASTER EGGS.

For bright Easter egg colors, combine ½ cup boiling water, 1 teaspoon vinegar, and 1 teaspoon food coloring. Dip eggs into the vinegar mixture until they are the color you desire.

PAINTING WITH VINEGAR.

Decorate finished or unfinished wooden picture frames, furniture, or other objects with a texturizing tool and a vinegar-paint solution. To make the paint, mix ½ cup white vinegar, 1 teaspoon granulated sugar, and a squeeze of clear liquid dish detergent. In a second container, place 2 tablespoons of dry powdered poster paint and enough vinegar solution to make a mixture that doesn't run when brushed on a vertical surface. Brush the solution on the surface, and with a texturing tool, such as a comb, a feather, a crumpled piece of paper, or a sponge, create the desired effect. Erase mistakes by wiping clean the surface with a rag moistened with distilled vinegar. When the painting is done, let it dry thoroughly, then apply several coats of clear polyurethane.

Child's Clay

2 cups flour
1 cup salt
1 teaspoon vinegar
½ cup water

Mix ingredients together and knead until soft. Divide into smaller portions and add a drop of food coloring if desired. To keep food coloring off hands, place the clay into a plastic bag before adding the food coloring. Store in the refrigerator.

Magic Apple Seeds

Kids get a kick out of this natural magic trick.

½ cup water
⅔ teaspoon baking soda
Seeds from 1 or more apples
1 tablespoon white vinegar

Pour the water into a clear drinking glass (a tall thin one works the best). Add the baking soda and stir until dissolved. Add the apple seeds, then the vinegar, and stir gently. The seeds will rise in the water as they are carried to the surface by carbon dioxide bubbles and then fall as the bubbles burst.

Easy Balloon Inflater

This is a simple way to fill balloons. Even older children enjoy this project and are amazed at how it works.

> *2 tablespoons water*
> *1 teaspoon baking soda*
> *1 clean empty soda bottle*
> *4 tablespoons white vinegar*

Stretch a balloon a few times to make it easier to inflate. Add the water and baking soda to the bottle. Add the vinegar and quickly fit the balloon over the top (mouth) of the bottle. The carbon dioxide released from the baking soda and vinegar mixture will inflate the balloon.

■ Vinegar for Beauty ■

VINEGAR BATH.
The restorative powers of a good long bath have been recognized since ancient times. Helen of Troy took vinegar baths. Adding ½ to 1 cup plain cider or herbal vinegar to bathwater helps you feel refreshed. Your skin responds favorably to having the proper acid, or pH, balance. Vinegar in the bathwater soothes, relaxes, cleanses, and removes itching or flaking skin. You can easily add herbs to a plain vinegar bath by placing fresh or dried herbs into a washcloth or a piece of cheesecloth and tying it shut. Toss the cloth with herbs into the bathwater.

Whether you add the herbs to the vinegar itself or place them into a cloth, try the delightful combinations below. When adding fresh herbs to the bath, use about ¼ cup or even more, if desired.

Suggested Vinegar Bath Combinations

- *Orange peel, rose petals, and peppermint leaves.*
- *Lavender flowers and rosemary leaves.*
- *Rose petals, almond oil, and witch hazel.*
- *Lemongrass and spearmint.*
- *Thyme, sage, and rose petals.*
- *Bay leaves and crushed cloves.*
- *Lemon peel and rose petals.*
- *Rose petals and chamomile flowers.*

Vinegar Bath Salts

4 cups vinegar
1 cup baking soda
½ cup Epsom salts
¼ cup salt

Mix well and store in a covered container. Use ½ cup for each bath. This will help relieve sore and tired muscles and make you feel energized.

BEAUTY VINEGARS.
These vinegar recipes can be used as a vinegar bath (add ½ to 1 cup to bathwater) or as a facial splash. (The truth be told, they can even be used as salad dressings!)

Herb Beauty Vinegar

1 quart apple cider vinegar
2 tablespoons fresh or dried herbs

Place vinegar in a glass or enamel pot and bring to a boil. Turn off heat and add herbs. Let cool and pour into a jar.

Mint Beauty Vinegar

This is my favorite beauty vinegar. In the bath it is refreshing, and a splash to the face always feels wonderful, especially during a long, hot summer.

> *1 handful fresh mint leaves*
> *1 quart apple cider vinegar*

Wash the mint, bruise its leaves well, and pack them into a jar filled with the vinegar. Cover tightly and let stand for 2 weeks. Strain out the mint and use. Note: Dried mint can be used, but you must first bring the vinegar to a boil before pouring it over the dried mint.

Rose Beauty Vinegar

> *1 pint apple cider vinegar*
> *1 ounce rose petals*
> *½ pint rose water*
> *1 ounce of lavender or sweet violet flowers*
> *1 ounce rosemary*

Mix ingredients together and steep for 2 weeks. Strain and use.

ENHANCE YOUR BODY WASH.

Add 1 tablespoon vinegar to liquid soaps designed for bathing. The vinegar will help remove soap residue and make your skin silky soft. After adding the vinegar, shake the bottle to mix the ingredients. Soak the body puff (or sponge) that comes with the liquid body wash in a solution of ¼ cup vinegar, 1 tablespoon baking soda, and 2 cups of hot water to remove dirt and any odor.

RELIEVE DRY SKIN.

Skin can get very dry any time of the year. Pour ½ cup baking soda and 1 cup vinegar into the bathwater for a refreshing bath. For extremely dry and itchy skin, add ½ cup oatmeal to the baking soda-and-vinegar bath. Oatmeal, vinegar, and baking soda will relive the itching at a low price.

REMOVE SOAP FILM.

Apple cider vinegar will remove soap scum from more than just the bathtub and shower. Mix a solution of half vinegar and half water and use it to rub down your body after bathing. It will feel terrific and leave your skin soft and free of soapy film. As an added bonus, it also acts as a natural deodorant.

SPONGE BATH.

When there's no time to take a bath or shower, take a quick vinegar sponge bath instead. Mix ½ cup vinegar in a quart of water. Dip a sponge or washcloth into the mixture for a quick cleanup. The vinegar water will neutralize odors and wash away dirt and perspiration.

CLEAN HANDS.

To clean and soften hands after cleaning the house or working in the garden, wash them with apple cider vinegar. Simply pour a little full-strength vinegar on your hands and rub them together. Rinse with clean water.

REMOVE BLEACH FROM HANDS.

After using household bleach products to clean around the house, your hands will feel slick. Get rid of that slick feeling and soften hands by washing them with soap and water and then applying vinegar.

RELIEVE SKIN IRRITATION.

Vinegar can soothe minor skin irritations (such as bug bites and sunburn). Just sponge full-strength vinegar on the skin for a quick relief.

SOFTEN HANDS.

Rub about 1 tablespoon of cider vinegar on your hands after taking a shower or bath or working in the kitchen. It will soften hands very nicely. It's a lot cheaper than hand lotions and not greasy.

EXTEND THE LIFE OF POLISHED NAILS.

Before applying nail polish, rub your fingernails with cotton balls that have been dipped in vinegar. This not only cleans them thoroughly but will help polish stay on longer.

DEODORIZE YOURSELF.

Vinegar is a natural deodorant that can replace deodorant sprays or creams. Simply splash full-strength vinegar under your arms and allow to dry. It will keep odor away for several hours and prevent deodorant stains on your clothes.

REPLACE FEMININE DEODORANTS.

Use a solution of 1 part vinegar and 3 parts water to wash instead of buying feminine towelettes.

FRESHEN BREATH.

A vinegar-and-salt rinse will eliminate breath odors caused by eating onions or garlic. In addition, this rinse is an excellent germ-killing gargle for a sore throat. Add 2 tablespoons of vinegar and 1 teaspoon of salt to 1 cup of warm water to make a rinse.

CLEAN DENTURES.

Soak dentures in white vinegar overnight to clean and deodorize them. Vinegar does a terrific job and costs a fraction of the price of a commercial denture cleaner.

CLEAN COMBS AND HAIRBRUSHES.

Soak plastic combs and hairbrushes overnight in a solution of 2 cups hot soapy water and ½ cup vinegar. In the morning, rinse and allow to dry. They will be clean as can be.

RELIEVE DANDRUFF.

Before spending big bucks on dandruff shampoo, try this home remedy. Beat 2 egg yolks in ½ cup of water and ¼ cup vinegar. Massage into the hair and scalp for five to ten minutes. Wash out with water and then rinse with a mixture of 2 tablespoons of apple cider vinegar and 1 cup water. Do this once every other week.

CLEAN EYEGLASSES.

Add a few drops of vinegar to 2 tablespoons of tap water. The vinegar water will make eyeglasses shine without streaks. Pour the vinegar-water solution into a tiny spray bottle, and you have a portable eyeglass cleaner. Or simply wipe each lens with a drop of vinegar for a streak-free shine.

CLEAN SILVER JEWELRY.

Soak silver jewelry in a solution of ½ cup of vinegar and 2 tablespoons baking soda for two hours. Rinse with water and buff to a shine.

CHECK CALCIUM SUPPLEMENTS.

To check how calcium supplements will be absorbed into your body, drop them into vinegar. If they dissolve quickly, then they are of good quality. Some calcium supplements will not dissolve and pass through your body without doing a bit of good. Always check the brand you buy to make sure you are not wasting your money.

Strawberry Vinegar Face Treatment

3 large or 5 small strawberries
⅓ cup vinegar

Mash the strawberries into the vinegar and let it sit for at least 2 hours or overnight. Strain the vinegar through a cloth. Before bedtime, pat the strawberry vinegar onto your face and neck. In the morning wash with a mild soap. This will help make your skin radiant and blemish free. The strawberry vinegar treatment will make you feel like you've been pampered at a spa.

Cider Facial Treatment

¼ cup cider vinegar
¼ cup water

Mix the cider and water together and gently wipe your face with the mixture. Let this vinegar treatment dry on your skin. Cider facial treatment will make your face feel soft and refreshed.

Herb Facial Splash

2 cups cider vinegar
⅓ cup honey
1 teaspoon sage
1 teaspoon thyme
1 teaspoon ground cloves
1 teaspoon crushed bay leaves

Combine all ingredients and store in a clean jar for 2 weeks. Shake the jar once or twice a day during the 2-week period to mix the contents. Strain the liquid and pour into a clean container with a tight cap.

After washing your face, pour some herb facial splash on your hands, pat on your face, and let dry on your skin.

CONDITION YOUR HAIR.
Vinegar is a natural hair conditioner, and it will bring out red highlights. Use vinegar as a rinse any time you notice a buildup of any type of hair product.

Vinegar Hair Rinse

Vinegar is one of the best hair rinses for all types of hair. It helps restore the natural acid balance of the scalp, stops itching, and helps control dandruff. It cleanses the hair and scalp.

⅓ cup white vinegar
½ cup water
2 tablespoons fresh or dried rosemary
2 tablespoons fresh or dried sage
2 tablespoons fresh or dried parsley
[For light hair: ¼ cup lemon juice]

Combine all ingredients and bring to a rolling boil in a glass or an enamel pot. Simmer uncovered for 15 minutes and then cover and let steep for 30 minutes.

Cool to room temperature, strain, and pour into a glass or plastic container. Vinegar hair rinse will keep for 2 to 3 months.

Use this rinse on hair after shampooing. Simply pour a small amount onto the hair and work it in with your fingertips. Rinse with cool water. Vinegar restores the natural acid balance to the hair and takes out any trace of soap.

To lighten hair or add highlights to light brown, red, or blond hair, add 2 tablespoons chamomile flowers. The flowers soften and lighten hair.

Dandruff Remedy Rinse

1 cup apple cider vinegar
5 aspirin tablets, crushed
⅓ cup witch hazel

Combine all ingredients and store in a tightly capped jar or bottle. After shampooing, gently massage dandruff remedy rinse into your hair and leave it on for 10 minutes. Rinse with warm water. Shake rinse before each use.

NOTE: Use only uncoated generic aspirin tablets, which dissolve quickly. Do not use coated tablets or caplets.

Tanning Oil

4 tea bags
½ cup water
1 cup wheat germ oil
¼ cup sesame oil
¼ cup apple cider vinegar
2 tablespoons aloe gel
1 teaspoon iodine
½ teaspoon almond extract

Boil the tea bags in ½ cup water. Allow the tea to steep for a few minutes. Squeeze out the teas bags into the water and discard the bags. In a small bowl, stir the oils and vinegar together, then gently beat in the aloe gel using a wire whisk. Add the tea, iodine, and extract, and pour into a tightly capped plastic container. Tanning oil will keep for about 3 months in the refrigerator.

NOTE: This formula is not recommended for children or people with fair skin. However, if you like to bake in the sun, despite all the health warnings, you'll like this natural substitute for commercial dark tanning oils.

Quick Cool Sunburn-Relief Formula

1 cup white vinegar
5 tablespoons salt
5 tablespoons plain yogurt
2 tablespoons aloe gel

Combine the ingredients and stir until the mixture is smooth and creamy. Pour into a jar and store in the refrigerator. Shake before using. Smooth the mixture on sunburned skin every hour until burning sensation is gone. Or try soaking a cloth in the sunburn mixture and gently laying it on the sore area to relieve the pain. This formula works wonders for mild cases of sunburn.

VINEGAR FORMULAS FOR HOUSEHOLD CLEANING

Instead of spending three to six dollars or even more per bottle for a cleaning product, you can make your own for a fraction of the cost without sacrificing quality. People have relied on natural formulas for years, and you'll find they work just as well as commercial products.

Before you start making homemade cleaning formulas, buy some spray bottles or save spray bottles from commercial cleaners when they are empty. You can find spray bottles for sale at discount stores, grocery stores, dollar stores, and even flea markets. Look for a package of three or six bottles for the best price. If you save spray bottles from a commercial product, always wash them out with hot soapy water and allow them to dry before using them for a homemade product. With a permanent black marker, write on the outside the contents of the bottle. Store your homemade formulas with the same care as you would any commercial formula; even though they are made from natural products, they should be kept out of the reach of small children.

Important note: When making your own cleaners, never combine chlorine bleach with vinegar, since it creates a harmful, potentially deadly gas.

Some ingredients (such as baking soda or soap) will make a white foam when added to vinegar. This is a natural chemical reaction that is not dangerous in an open container. Do not seal a vinegar mixture that is foaming in a tightly capped container. Let the foam die down before closing the top.

As with all other cleaning products, these homemade vinegar formulas need to be tested before using them. Always try them on a small hidden area of the clothes, carpet, upholstery, or whatever you are cleaning. While most of these formulas are not as harsh as commercial cleaning products, it's better to be safe than sorry.

NOTE: Vinegar can dissolve preexisting wax on furniture and floors. Use very small amounts or diluted formulas to clean and shine; use stronger solutions to remove wax buildup and heavy dirt.

For generations our forefathers (or maybe "foremothers") have been combining vinegar with other household supplies to clean all around the house. Store-bought cleaners are not always as environmentally safe as natural, organic compounds. Most homemade cleaning formulas can be made for a fraction of the cost of a commercial counterpart. A number of substances are combined with vinegar to make the formulas below; here are some general guidelines to the more popular mixtures.

To vinegar add:

- baking soda to absorb odors, deodorize, and create a mild abrasive
- borax to disinfect, deodorize, and stop the growth of mold
- chalk for a mild, nonabrasive cleaner
- oil to preserve, polish, and shine
- pumice to remove tough stains or polish surfaces
- salt for a mild abrasive
- washing soda to cut heavy grease
- wax to protect and shine

ALL-PURPOSE CLEANER

½ cup household ammonia
½ cup white vinegar
¼ cup baking soda
½ gallon of water

Combine ingredients in a glass or plastic bottle. This formula works for all sorts of general cleaning chores. Pour some into a spray bottle to keep handy.

ALL-PURPOSE BATH CLEANER

½ cup vinegar
1 cup clear ammonia
¼ cup baking soda
1 gallon warm water

Mix together and use to clean bathroom fixtures, walls, and countertops. This formula is a particularly effective soap-scum remover. Pour some of the mixture into a spray bottle. Use the rest of the formula straight from the bucket to clean all around the bathroom. Rinse with clean water.

TOILET BOWL CLEANER

1 cup vinegar
1 cup borax

Pour the vinegar in the toilet bowl, working some up around the rim. Sprinkle the borax over the vinegar. Allow the mixture to soak for at least 2 hours or leave it on overnight. Use a brush to loosen the grime, then flush.

CERAMIC-TILE AND GROUT CLEANER

1 cup baking soda
1 cup household ammonia
½ cup vinegar
warm water

Pour baking soda into a clean gallon-size plastic jug. Add ammonia, vinegar, and enough warm water to fill the jug about half full. Shake the jug to mix the ingredients together. Add more warm water to fill the jug. Pour some of the solution into a spray bottle, spray directly on the tiles, and wipe clean with a sponge. Rinse with water. Be sure to put the cap on the jug tightly. Label and keep out of the reach of small children.

HEAVY-DUTY GROUT CLEANER

2 tablespoons baking soda
1 tablespoon vinegar
2 tablespoons Ceramic-Tile and Grout Cleaner (recipe
    above)

Mix the ingredients to make a paste. Use an old toothbrush to apply to the grout. Let the paste soak into the grout for 10 minutes, then scrub with the toothbrush and rinse with water.

KITCHEN GREASE-CUTTING CLEANER

¼ cup baking soda
⅔ cup white vinegar
¾ cup ammonia
hot water

Pour the first three ingredients into a clean gallon container. Shake to mix. Add enough hot water to fill the container. Use the cleaner to wash greasy areas in the kitchen. Rinse with clean water and let dry. To protect your hands, use rubber gloves and make sure you have adequate ventilation in the room.

OVEN CLEANER

1 cup vinegar
1 cup borax
¼ cup concentrated powdered laundry detergent

Make a paste out of the vinegar, borax, and detergent. Heat the oven to 400 degrees for 5 minutes and turn off. Spread the paste all over the oven and leave it on for at least an hour. Scrape the gook off with a spatula or an expired credit card. This formula works best for light to medium cleaning. It won't be perfect, but it will be safer than commercial sprays. When used often, this formula easily removes the food particles.

CALCIUM DEPOSIT REMOVER

Use this formula to remove tough calcium or mineral deposits that develop inside a teapot or kettle.

1 tablespoon white vinegar
1 cup water

Simmer the water and vinegar in the pot for 30 minutes. Once the deposits are loosened, you can scrub them out with a brush or steel wool pad. If you cannot get to the deposits, let the mixture soak overnight, rinse, and repeat the process if necessary. For heavy deposits, drop a marble into the kettle to help loosen the tough deposits. The marble will move around in the boiling water, chipping off the mineral deposits.

AUTOMATIC COFFEEMAKER CLEANER

1 cup white vinegar
1 cup water

Mix the vinegar and water.

For automatic coffeemakers, put in a new coffee filter and pour the solution directly into the water reservoir. Turn on the coffeemaker and let the vinegar and water run through. Save this hot vinegar water solution in another container to clean the outside of the coffeemaker and coffeepot. Remove the coffee filter. Fill the reservoir with clean tap water and run the coffeemaker through another cycle. Discard this water.

NONSTICK COOKWARE CLEANER

½ cup white vinegar
2 tablespoons baking soda
1 cup warm water

Mix the ingredients together and pour into nonstick pans. Place on the stove and boil for 10 minutes. Maintain adequate ventilation by opening a window or using the stove hood fan. Wash in soapy water and rinse well.

BRASS POLISH

1 cup powdered laundry detergent
2 tablespoons salt
¼ cup white vinegar
4 cups boiling water

Mix powdered laundry detergent and salt together in a glass or an enamel pan. Stir in vinegar and slowly add the boiling water until the soap is dissolved. Let cool. Pour into a clean glass jar and cover tightly. Label and keep out of the reach of children.

To use, shake well and pour about 1 teaspoon of the solution onto a soft cloth and then apply to the brass piece. Rub gently, turning the rag often. Apply more of the solution until the tarnish is gone. Buff with a clean, dry cloth until brass is dry and shiny.

COPPER CLEANER

½ cup flour
½ cup salt
½ cup powdered laundry detergent
¾ cup white vinegar
¼ cup lemon juice
½ cup hot water (not boiling)

In a glass bowl mix together the ingredients, making sure the soap dissolves. Pour into a clean glass jar and cover tightly. Label and keep out of children's reach.

To use, shake the solution and pour some of the mixture onto the copper piece. Then gently scrub with a sponge. Rinse with water, let dry, and buff with a soft cloth.

METAL CLEANER

This cleaner works especially well on stainless steel, but it can be used for any type of metal.

2 tablespoons cream of tartar
vinegar

Combine the cream of tartar and enough vinegar to make a paste. Rub the paste on and let it dry. Wash it off with warm water and buff with a soft, dry towel. This will make metals shine like new.

PEWTER CLEANER

1 tablespoon salt
1 tablespoon flour
vinegar

Mix salt and flour together and add enough vinegar to just dampen the mixture. Smear the paste on discolored pewter and allow to dry. Rub the dried paste off, rinse in hot water, and buff dry.

NOTE: Pewter also cleans up easily if rubbed with cabbage leaves. Simply wet the leaves in vinegar and dip them in salt before using them to buff the pewter. Rinse with water and dry thoroughly.

SUPER-DUPER STAIN REMOVER
(LAUNDRY PREWASH)

½ cup vinegar
½ cup ammonia
¼ cup baking soda
2 tablespoons liquid detergent
2 quarts water

Mix together in a clean container with a lid. Shake until well mixed; pour into a spray bottle. Spray the solution on stains and let it soak in for a few minutes before washing as usual.

INK STAIN-REMOVER FORMULA

1 tablespoon white vinegar
1 tablespoon milk
1 teaspoon borax
1 teaspoon lemon juice

Mix the ingredients together and apply to the ink spot. Wait a few minutes and sponge off the mixture with cool water. Repeat until the stain is gone.

FABRIC SOFTENER

2 cups baking soda
1 cup white vinegar
4 cups water

Mix ingredients together and store in a plastic or glass container with a tight lid in the laundry room. Label the container and keep out of children's reach.

To use, shake ingredients to mix, then add ¼ cup to the final rinse in your washing machine.

NOTE: You can make a scented fabric softener by using herb vinegar instead of white vinegar.

■ Window Cleaners ■

Several variations of window cleaner can be made at home.

WINDOW CLEANER FORMULA 1

1 tablespoon of vinegar
2 cups of water
2 drops of blue food coloring, if desired

Mix together and pour into a spray bottle. Shake to mix before using.

NOTE: The food coloring does not facilitate cleaning, but the blue color makes the solution look like the commercial product.

WINDOW CLEANER FORMULA 2

2 tablespoons of vinegar
4 tablespoons of ammonia
2 cups of water
2 drops of blue food coloring, if desired

Mix together and pour into a spray bottle. Shake to mix before using.

WINDOW CLEANER FORMULA 3

¼ cup vinegar
¼ cup ammonia
1 tablespoon of cornstarch
1½ cups of water
2 drops of blue food coloring, if desired

Mix together and pour into a spray bottle. Shake to mix before using.

HANDY WINDOW CLEANER

½ teaspoon liquid soap
¼ cup vinegar
2 cups water

Dip a sponge or small cloth into this formula, then wring it out. Store the window-cleaning cloth in a jar with a tight-fitting lid or a heavy (freezer type) plastic bag with a zipper-type closing. Then when needed, wipe spots and smears from dirty windows. They will clean up easily without streaks. You'll want to put one in the house and another in the car. Save the formula in a jar and dip the sponge or rag back into the mixture as needed.

MIRROR CLEANER

1 tablespoon vinegar
3 tablespoons household ammonia
2 cups water

Mix together vinegar, household ammonia, and water. Pour into a spray bottle.

SCOURING POWDER 1

½ cup baking soda
¼ cup vinegar

Mix baking soda and vinegar to the consistency of paste. Apply to dirty surfaces and let sit for 30 minutes. Sponge clean with water.

SCOURING POWDER 2

For really tough stains try this formula, but be careful not to scratch the surface you are cleaning.

¼ cup vinegar
¼ cup salt
¼ cup flour

Mix together to make a paste. Use a soft cloth to apply, then rinse with clear water. Buff with another soft cloth.

SCOURING LIQUID

Liquid scouring cleaners have become a popular alternative to regular powdered cleaners; they are convenient to use and easy to make. Here's how:

> ¼ cup baking soda
> 1 tablespoon liquid dishwashing detergent
> vinegar

Mix the baking soda and liquid dishwashing detergent and add enough vinegar to make a creamy liquid. Pour into a clean plastic squeeze bottle, and you have a low-cost alternative to the liquid scouring cleaners.

VINEGAR AIR-FRESHENER SPRAY

> 1 teaspoon baking soda
> 1 tablespoon vinegar
> 2 cups water

Mix together in a spray bottle. The mixture will foam quite a bit. When it stops foaming, put on the lid and shake well. Spray this mixture into the air for instant freshness. This is an environmentally friendly air freshener that is also very inexpensive. Make one for each bathroom and for the kitchen. It eliminates odors without any gagging fake smells.

SCENTED VINEGAR AIR-FRESHENER SPRAY

> 2 cups white vinegar
> 1 cup dried or fresh herbs or spices (see list for herb and
>   spice suggestions)
> ½ teaspoon peppermint extract or vanilla extract (if
>   desired)

You can tailor this recipe to suit your taste by adding the herbs and spices that you like to smell. I suggest: cloves, rose petals, thyme, rosemary, cinnamon sticks, pine needles, lemon, lime, apple or orange peel, honeysuckle, or other fragrant flower blossoms.

Place all ingredients in a glass or enamel pan. Bring the mixture to a boil and simmer over low heat for 10 minutes. Cool. Pour liquid and herbs into a large glass jar. Close the jar tightly. Shake the jar once or twice a week for 4 weeks. If the jar has a metal lid, place a piece of plastic wrap over the top of the jar before screwing on the lid. After 4 weeks, strain and reserve juice. Pour liquid into a pump spray container and spray into the air to freshen it.

VINYL CLEANER

½ cup vinegar
2 teaspoons liquid soap
½ cup water

Combine well and use a soft cloth to wipe this mixture onto vinyl furniture. Then rinse with clean water and buff dry.

WALL CLEANER

¼ cup baking soda
½ cup white vinegar
1 cup household ammonia
1 gallon hot water

Mix together and use a sponge to clean the dirt, grime, and fingerprints off walls. When washing walls, start from the bottom and work your way up so drips of dirty water will not run down dry walls. Rinse with clean water.

MILDEW CLEANER

½ cup white vinegar
½ cup liquid soap
¼ cup salt

Apply to mildew stains on tile floors, walls, and window ledges and leave in a well-ventilated place for 2 hours. Wash and rinse well.

CARPET CLEANER

1 tablespoon white vinegar
1 tablespoon household ammonia
1 quart water

Mix vinegar, ammonia, and water together. Apply to spots on the carpet with a soft rag. Rinse with clean water and allow to dry. Use a fan to speed drying time.

VARNISH REMOVER

This works great for wood floors, furniture, and woodwork. It is inexpensive to make and less toxic than commercial products.

1 cup cornstarch
½ cup cold water
1 quart boiling water
¾ cup baking soda
½ cup ammonia
1 tablespoon vinegar

Mix cornstarch and cold water. Add boiling water, baking soda, ammonia, and vinegar. Apply with a paintbrush while the mixture is still hot. Rewarm the varnish remover if necessary. After varnish loosens, wash off with a cloth and hot water.

WOOD CLEANER 1

Perfect for wood paneling, doors, furniture, cupboards. This is the best formula for the routine cleaning of wood.

> *1 quart warm water*
> *1 teaspoon vinegar*
> *1 teaspoon olive oil*

Mix together. Dip a soft cloth into the mixture and wring it out. Use this cloth to wipe the wood surface. Polish with a soft, dry cloth.

WOOD CLEANER 2

Use this wood formula to remove heavy dirt or to clean up an old piece of furniture.

> *1 cup boiled linseed oil*
> *1 cup turpentine*
> *1 cup vinegar*
> *1 quart warm water*

Mix in a pail and use a rag to rub into the wood.

"MAGIC" FURNITURE POLISH

> *¼ cup linseed oil*
> *⅛ cup vinegar*
> *⅛ cup whiskey*

Mix together and use a soft rag to polish furniture. The dirt seems to disappear magically as the alcohol evaporates.

WOODWORM FURNITURE CONDITIONER

If you have a problem with woodworms, use this formula on your wood furniture. Apply once a year.

> ½ cup linseed oil
> ½ cup turpentine
> ¼ cup vinegar
> ¼ cup rubbing alcohol

Pour into a glass jar and shake well. Apply with a clean, soft cloth to wood furniture.

SADDLE SOAP

> ¼ cup beeswax
> ¼ cup vinegar
> 2 tablespoons liquid soap
> 2 tablespoons linseed oil

Warm the beeswax slowly in the vinegar. Then add the soap and oil. Keep the mixture warm until it mixes together smoothly. Pour into a small metal tin. Then let cool until solid. To use, rub it onto leather, then buff to a high shine.

LEATHER CLEANER

> 1 tablespoon vinegar
> 1 tablespoon alcohol
> 1 teaspoon vegetable oil
> ½ teaspoon liquid soap

Mix together. Work this into shoes or other leather items such as purses or car seats, then shine with a soft cloth or brush.

Floor Cleaner

¼ cup liquid soap
½ cup vinegar
2 gallons of warm water

Mix together and use to mop wood, tile, or linoleum floors.

OLD-FASHIONED
VINEGAR FOLK REMEDIES

Apple cider vinegar reportedly lowers blood pressure and facilitates circulation. It helps remove built-up calcium in joints and blood vessels without interfering with the calcium in teeth and bones. This helps fight against kidney stones, arthritis, bursitis, and tendinitis. Vinegar contains nineteen of the twenty-two minerals essential for human health. The benefits of vinegar are also reported to include a strong and regular heartbeat, a healthy digestive system, and good working kidneys.

Vinegar has been used to cure ailments for centuries. For hundreds of years, folk medicine practitioners have recommended daily doses of apple cider vinegar, not only for specific medical problems, but for overall good heath. In the old days, people weren't aware of cancer, antioxidants, or free radicals, but they recognized that something in apple cider vinegar helped prevent disease and kept them active and healthy into old age. Skeptics thought that vinegar folk remedies were just old wives' tales, but research has shown that apple cider vinegar has some extraordinary healing abilities.

Folk medicine has found many different uses for apple cider vinegar. These home remedies may change slightly as they are passed down from one generation to the next, but one thing always stays the same—the belief that even a small amount of apple cider vinegar taken daily contributes to a longer, more active, and healthier life.

■ Wholesome Organic Vinegar ■

As strange as it sounds, vinegar can actually be made from wood shavings. But it cannot be expected to have the same balance of healthful vitamins and minerals as vinegar made from apples. And vinegar made from only apple cores and peelings cannot be expected to have the same taste and nutritional value as vinegar made from fresh whole eating apples. The very best, most wholesome apple cider vinegar is made from whole apples that have no pesticide residue on them.

A high-quality apple cider vinegar is packed full of healthy enzymes, amino acids, vitamins, and minerals. This is true only if it has been produced with care, from whole, good-quality apples that have not been treated with toxic chemicals.

WHAT IS ORGANIC?

An organic food is one that is grown without chemical fertilizers, herbicides, or pesticides that can end up in the final product. An organic apple grower uses only natural fertilizers to stimulate growth and employs alternative methods to keep bugs away. Organic growing can be difficult, but it results in much healthier food. I have found that organically grown foods are more flavorful than those that have been chemically treated, and I don't have to worry about potential health problems that can be caused by these chemicals.

Many producers of organic vinegars proudly display their organic status, along with other helpful information, on their label, for example, "This unfiltered, raw, organic apple cider vinegar was made in the traditional way, from whole, ripe organically grown apples that were pressed and naturally fermented.

Shake well before using. Organically grown and processed in a manner that far exceeds the requirements of the California Organic Foods Act of 1990." Some labels even state the location of the orchard. If the label of an organic apple cider vinegar does not say that *whole apples* are used, you can assume that the vinegar is made from cores and peelings.

The Federal Organic Production Act of 1990, which went into effect in 1993, established strict guidelines for a grower to qualify for the organic certification. One important mandate was that a harvest cannot be certified organic unless the land the product grows on has not been treated with synthetics for three years. Organic certification assures consumers that foods labeled organic have been grown, processed, or handled in compliance with standards designed to keep the food, as well as agricultural workers and the environment, free of harmful contaminants.

What's so Important about Organic?

Everyone experiences the wear and tear of time on their body. Scientists tell us that much of what we call aging is damage caused by free radicals that bounce through our body, damaging cells and causing them to mutate. If we eat the right kinds of wholesome foods, many free radicals are absorbed, thus minimizing their damage. The better job we do of providing the building blocks of a healthful body, the better we can retain the vitality and energy of youth. Apples contain these very building blocks. Pure, unfiltered, apple cider vinegar combines the natural goodness of apples with amino acids and enzymes created in the fermentation process. They remain in the vinegar if it is not filtered, overheated, pasteurized, or overprocessed. Organic raw apple cider vinegar can be an important part of a long, healthy life.

Pretty or Healthy?

Sometimes, in their haste to market a vinegar, companies process apples with chemicals that speed up the fermentation process. Or, to cut costs, they substitute culls and apple by-products (such as cores and peels) for the whole fruit. Many vinegars are subjected to excessive heat and processed with preservatives and clarifying agents, which may make for a "pretty" vinegar product but it also sacrifices some of the healthy properties present in an organically produced vinegar.

WHERE TO BUY ORGANIC VINEGAR

Some grocery stores are starting to carry organic apple cider vinegar because customers are asking for it. Keep in mind that if the label does not specifically state that the vinegar is organic, it is not organic. You can usually find an assortment of organic vinegars at health food stores in small bottles and probably even in gallon jugs. In addition to apple cider vinegar, health food stores generally carry other organic vinegars in natural flavors such as peach, raspberry, and mango. You'll pay a little more for organic vinegar, but if you are using it for health reasons, the extra money is worth it. If you want to treat yourself to something special that's not fattening—and is actually good for you— try a good-quality organically produced, apple cider vinegar!

PICKING AN ORGANIC VINEGAR

The best apple cider vinegar is made by giving meticulous attention to producing a consistent, high-quality product. It is not diluted with water and can take a full four to six weeks to produce. High-quality vinegar is aged in wood barrels, not plastic or metal ones.

Look for sediment. At the bottom of all bottles of organic vinegars lie pectin and apple residues, which are packed with nutrients. If you see no sediment, the very best part of the vinegar has probably been filtered out. This kind of vinegar will be full-flavored and have a strong apple aroma, yet not be overly sour.

Make sure the vinegar was made from whole apples (not merely culls, peels, or cores) that were organically grown on soil with a high mineral content (such as land in the northern United States). The label should state that a third party has monitored the vinegar's organic status.

■ Home Remedies ■

These vinegar home remedies are not meant to take the place of your family doctor. Before using any remedy, you should discuss your medical condition with your family doctor, and if symptoms persists or worsen, make your doctor aware of the problem and ask for advice on how to alleviate it.

Home remedies are listed in alphabetical order by ailment or condition, so you can use this section as a handy reference.

ACNE.
Make a mixture of 2 teaspoons apple cider vinegar and 1 cup of water to dab on blemishes several times a day after washing. The vinegar treatment will help clear up the acne without drying out the skin.

ACTIVE LIFESTYLE.
Maintain a healthy and active lifestyle well into old age by making a vinegar tonic to drink before each meal. Combine 1 teaspoon vinegar and 1 tablespoon honey into 1 cup of water.

AGE SPOTS.
Age spots (liver spots) can be faded or even eliminated with onion juice and vinegar. Mix 1 teaspoon onion juice (squeezed from a fresh onion) and 2 teaspoons vinegar together and rub on the spots once or twice a day. In a few weeks the spots will begin to fade.

ARTHRITIS.
To alleviate arthritis pain, drink a glass full of water with 2 tablespoons of apple cider vinegar before each meal and at bedtime.

ATHLETE'S FOOT.
Athlete's foot can be relieved by soaking socks or stockings in vinegar water. Combine 1 part vinegar and 4 parts water; soak the socks for 30 minutes before washing as usual. Relieve the

itching of athlete's foot by rinsing the feet several times a day with undiluted apple cider vinegar.

BACKACHES.
For a sore back, add 2 cups of apple cider vinegar to your bathwater. Soak for twenty minutes. Add ½ cup of baking soda or 1 cup Epsom salts for added relief.

BAD BREATH.
Gargle with a solution of half vinegar and half water. If desired, use mint vinegar for a fresh-tasting mouthwash.

BEE OR JELLYFISH STING.
To soothe a bee or jellyfish sting, mix a solution of 3 parts vinegar (white or apple cider) to 1 part water and apply to the sting. It will soothe the skin irritation and relieve itching.

BLADDER INFECTIONS.
To reduce the chances of getting a bladder infection, take a small amount of vinegar each day. The vinegar helps keep the urinary tract at the proper acid level.

BOILS.

Old-Time Home Remedy for Boils

Try this homemade liniment for use on boils.

> 1 cup vinegar
> ¼ cup turpentine
> white of 1 fresh egg

Combine the ingredients in a bottle and shake until they are mixed. The mixture will have a white creamy texture. Apply a small amount to boils on the skin and allow to dry. Repeat twice daily. If your skin is sensitive, omit the turpentine.

BRUISES.
Dip onion slices into apple cider vinegar and rub on bruises immediately after they occur to prevent black-and-blue marks from forming.

BUG BITES.
Itchy skin irritations such as mosquito bites, insect and bee stings, welts, and hives can be relieved with a paste of vinegar and cornstarch. To make a paste, start with 2 tablespoons of cornstarch and keep adding vinegar drop by drop until it is the consistency of a paste. Just pat the vinegar-and-cornstarch paste on the area and let it dry. The paste will help draw out the poison and prevent swelling.

BURNS.
To alleviate the pain of minor burns, pat undiluted cold apple cider vinegar on the burned area every fifteen minutes. Keep a bottle of apple cider vinegar in the refrigerator to use for this purpose.

Cholesterol-Lowering Drink

2 cups cranberry juice
2 cups white grape juice
2 cups apple juice
⅓ cup apple cider vinegar

Mix all the ingredients together and drink one 8-ounce glass each morning and evening. Many people reportedly lowered their cholesterol levels significantly by drinking this mixture. The vinegar is the "secret" ingredient for lowering cholesterol.

COLD RELIEF.
Soak a cotton handkerchief in apple cider vinegar. Sprinkle black pepper on the cloth and bind it to the chest with a towel. Place the pepper side of the cloth next to the skin. After twenty min-

utes, remove the cloth and wash the chest, being careful not to get chilled. Repeat twice a day.

CORNS AND CALLUSES.

Use a vinegar compress to remove corns and calluses. Soak a slice of stale bread in apple cider vinegar; tear off a piece of the bread large enough to cover the corn or callus and tape it in place with first-aid tape. Leave the bread on the area overnight, and in the morning you'll see a big difference.

COUGH REMEDY.

To ease a dry hacking cough that keeps you awake at night, sprinkle your pillowcase with apple cider vinegar.

DANDRUFF.

Eliminate dandruff and make hair healthy by rinsing after each shampoo with one-half cup apple cider vinegar mixed with 2 cups of water.

DIARRHEA.

To prevent traveler's diarrhea, drink a mixture of 1 teaspoon apple cider vinegar, 1 teaspoon honey, and 2 cups water thirty minutes before each meal. If traveling out of the country, be sure to use bottled water instead of tap water. Start this treatment a few days before traveling and continue during your stay away from home.

DIGESTION.

Good health often depends on good digestion. Apple cider vinegar can keep your digestive system in top shape because apple cider vinegar destroys the bacteria, fungi, and viruses that can make you sick. Drink 2 cups of water with 2 tablespoons of apple cider vinegar at each meal. You can add honey to the vinegar water, if desired.

DIZZINESS.
To prevent dizziness or reduce its severity, drink a vinegar-and-honey "cocktail." Mix 2 teaspoons cider vinegar and 2 teaspoons honey into ½ cup of warm water. Drink the mixture twice a day. This will lessen your symptoms but probably will not completely eliminate the dizziness all together.

DOUCHE.
Frequent douching is no longer recommended for women, but if you are prone to vaginal infections, you can prevent them by occasionally douching with a solution of 2 teaspoons apple cider vinegar and 1 quart of warm water.

EARACHES.
To treat earaches and swimmer's ear, mix together equal parts of vinegar and rubbing alcohol. Apply a couple of drops in each ear as needed.

FATIGUE (CHRONIC).
For relief of chronic fatigue, add 3 teaspoons of apple cider vinegar to a cup of honey. Take 2 teaspoons of the mixture before going to bed each evening. This should perk you up and give you more energy the next day.

Flu Remedy

¼ cup honey
¼ cup apple cider vinegar

Mix together and take 1 tablespoon every 4 hours or as needed.

FRECKLES.
Lighten freckles on the body (not the face) by rubbing full-strength vinegar on them. They will lighten over a period of several weeks. Freckles will not disappear completely, but you'll notice the difference.

FRIZZY HAIR.

Permed or curly hair will not be as frizzy if you rinse with a mixture of vinegar and water after shampooing and conditioning your hair. Combine 1 cup vinegar and 1 cup water. Pour on your hair and wait two minutes before rinsing with clean water.

GAS PAINS.

To ease gas pains, drink a glass of very warm water with 1 teaspoon honey and 1 teaspoon vinegar added.

HEADACHES.

Add ¼ cup apple cider vinegar to the water in a vaporizer and inhale the vapors for five to ten minutes. Rest quietly, and the headache should go away in about thirty minutes or less. This helps to relieve migraines.

HEADACHES (CHRONIC).

If you suffer from chronic headaches, try taking 1 tablespoon of vinegar each morning and evening and before breakfast and dinner. If headaches are very painful increase the dosage to 2 tablespoons.

HEADACHES (SINUS).

Drink a glass of water with 1 teaspoon of apple cider vinegar five times during the day to ease the pain and help clear the sinuses.

HEARTBURN.

To avoid heartburn, mix 1 teaspoon of apple cider vinegar in ½ glass of water and sip it throughout the meal.

HEART DISEASE.

To help prevent heart disease, drink 1 teaspoon of apple cider vinegar mixed with 1 cup apple cider or apple juice three times a day.

HEMORRHOIDS.
Bleeding hemorrhoids can be made less severe by drinking a vinegar-and-honey "cocktail." Mix 2 teaspoons of cider vinegar and 2 teaspoons of honey into ½ cup of warm water. Drink the mixture at every meal.

HICCUPS.
To get rid of a tough case of hiccups, sip a glass of warm water with 1 teaspoon of vinegar added. Drink the whole glass all at once, but slowly, and the hiccups should be gone.

IMPETIGO, RINGWORM, AND SHINGLES.
To help the skin heal, apply full-strength apple cider vinegar to the problem skin areas five or six times daily.

INSECT REPELLENT.
Keep insects and bees away when outdoors by rubbing vinegar on your body. Rub full-strength on any exposed parts such as arms, legs, wrists, ankles, and throat.

INSOMNIA.
For relief of insomnia, add 3 teaspoons of apple cider vinegar to a cup of honey. Take 2 teaspoons of the mixture before going to bed each evening. This will help you go to sleep. If you wake up in the middle of the night and can't go back to sleep, take another 2 teaspoons.

ITCHY SKIN.
Relieve itchy skin by patting undiluted apple cider vinegar on the area. If the itch is near the eyes or other delicate area, dilute the vinegar to 4 parts water and 1 part vinegar. The easiest way to treat large areas of itchy skin is to bathe in a vinegar bath. Simply add 2 or 3 cups of vinegar to the bathwater.

JOINT PAIN RELIEVER.
Many people claim that arthritis or other types of joint pain can be eased when they drink a vinegar-and-honey "cocktail." Mix 2

teaspoons of cider vinegar and 2 teaspoons of honey into ½ cup of warm water. Drink the mixture three times a day.

KIDNEY INFECTIONS.
To reduce the chances of getting a kidney infection, take 2 teaspoons of vinegar each day. The vinegar helps keep the urinary tract at the proper acid level. You can take the vinegar undiluted or mix it with 1 cup water and 2 tablespoons honey.

LEG CRAMPS.
Use cider vinegar to relieve leg cramps. Keep a spray bottle filled with undiluted vinegar next to your bed; then when you have a sudden attack of cramps you can reach for the bottle and get quick relief. Vinegar will stop the cramps in seconds. Nighttime leg cramps can be prevented by drinking a glass of water with 1 tablespoon of apple cider vinegar added to it before each meal.

LONG, HEALTHY LIFE.
To live a long and healthy life, drink organic apple cider vinegar every day. Simply add a tablespoon of vinegar to a glass of water and drink it at least once a day.

MEMORY.
Memory can be sharpened by drinking a glass of warm water with a teaspoon of apple cider vinegar added to it. Drink a glass with each meal.

MENSTRUAL CRAMPS.
Soak in a hot bath with 2 cups of cider vinegar.

MORNING SICKNESS.
To relieve morning sickness, drink a glass of water with 1 teaspoon of apple cider vinegar and 1 tablespoon of honey each morning and evening.

MOUTH SORES.

Swish vinegar around in your mouth to help speed the healing of mouth sores and swollen gums. You can use full-strength vinegar or dilute it with water.

NAUSEA, VOMITING.

Relieve the discomfort of nausea or vomiting by soaking a cloth in warm apple cider vinegar, wringing it out, and placing it on the stomach. Replace with another warm cloth when it cools. If you wake up nauseated or vomiting, drink a solution of water and 2 tablespoons of apple cider vinegar during the day. By evening you should feel like trying a light amount of food. Continue to take vinegar and water five times a day for the next three days to make sure the bacteria is completely out of your system.

NIGHT SWEATS.

Before going to bed, rub full-strength vinegar on your arms, legs, chest, neck, and shoulders. Allow to air-dry. Do not wash off. Many people find that this prevents night sweats or decreases their severity.

NOSEBLEEDS.

Hold a clean cotton cloth or gauze that has been dipped into white vinegar over your nose whenever you have a nosebleed. The vinegar will help stop the bleeding and speed the healing process.

PERSPIRATION ON HANDS.

If your hands are always moist from perspiration, bathe them in a weak solution of vinegar, which will act as an astringent. Mix 1 part vinegar with 4 or 5 parts water.

POISON IVY REMEDY 1.

To stop the itch of poison ivy, mix ½ vinegar and ½ water; dab frequently on infected area. It helps stop the itching and promotes healing.

POISON IVY REMEDY 2.

Mix 1 cup vinegar with 2 tablespoons salt in a saucepan. Boil until the salt is dissolved. Cool the mixture. Apply liberally to skin. Let dry and leave on the skin for at least thirty minutes. Reapply several times a day.

POSTNASAL DRIP.

To reduce postnasal drip, add 1 tablespoon of vinegar to a glass of water and drink once a day with a meal. You should notice a difference in about two weeks.

POTASSIUM DEFICIENCY.

Many common medical problems such as fatigue, memory loss, and high blood pressure can be caused by a potassium deficiency. Potassium promotes cell and tissue growth. To maintain an ideal level of potassium, there is no better source than organic apple cider vinegar. Incorporate apple cider vinegar into your diet by making a salad dressing with it or drinking a glass of water with 2 tablespoons of vinegar and 2 tablespoons of honey.

Many people have a potassium deficiency and don't even realize it. Older people with low potassium can experience premature aging such as hair loss, tooth decay, or weak, brittle fingernails. As we get older, we often need an increased amount of potassium to sustain new cell growth. Keep in mind that coffee, sugar, and alcohol can weaken the effects of potassium. If you drink beverages containing these substances and are frequently fatigued, you may have a potassium depletion.

HERE ARE SOME MORE SYMPTOMS THAT MAY INDICATE A POTASSIUM DEFICIENCY:

1. Trouble falling asleep at night; or staying asleep all night long.
2. Difficulty relaxing.
3. Loss of mental alertness that may include impatience, difficulty with decision-making, lapses in memory, or bouts of depression.

4. Skin bruises easily and the bruises are slow to heal.
5. Skin tends to itch frequently.
6. Increased tooth decay.
7. Muscle cramps in the legs, especially at night.
8. Calluses and corns on the feet.
9. Temporary loss of appetite, possibly with nausea and vomiting.
10. Soreness in joints or arthritis.
11. Skin is very sensitive to cold, especially the hands and feet.
12. Constipation.
13. Frequent colds and other types of sickness.
14. Loss of stamina and increased fatigue.
15. Lower back pain.
16. Dull headache in the morning, which may continue for several hours after waking, or it may go away quickly.

If you have five of more of these symptoms, you may have a potassium deficiency. It is best to see your doctor to be sure. There are several potassium-rich foods in addition to apple cider vinegar that you can eat: grape juice, apple juice, cranberry juice, bananas, grapefruit and other citrus fruits, paprika, potatoes, tomatoes, spinach, raw carrots, dark leafy greens, and sunflower seeds.

RINGWORM.
See Impetigo.

SCALP ITCH.
Add 1 tablespoon of vinegar to a glass of water and dip the comb into the mixture. Comb through the hair. Continue to do this until the hair and scalp are saturated with the vinegar water. This will help stop itching by returning the skin to its normal pH balance.

SHINGLES.
See Impetigo.

SHINY HAIR.

Vinegar adds a healthy shine to hair. It makes dark hair look richer, and it brings out the highlights in light hair. Vinegar especially makes gray hair shine. After shampooing, rinse your hair with ½ cup apple cider vinegar mixed with 2 cups of water.

SKIN IRRITATION: VINEGAR-AND-EGGSHELL LINIMENT.

In a small glass jar, place the two halves of an eggshell. Add enough apple cider vinegar to completely cover the eggshell. Screw on the lid tightly. Bubbles will start to form on the eggshell and within a day or two the eggshell will have dissolved into the vinegar. All the calcium and minerals from the eggshell are now in the vinegar mixture left in the jar. Apply the liniment to skin irritations, itchy skin, and sore, aching muscles.

SKIN IRRITATIONS.

If you have a skin irritation, sponge the area with undiluted vinegar. If the itching stops, the condition is on the outside of the skin, and the vinegar will quickly heal it. If the irritation persists, the condition may be internal; consult a doctor in that case. Applying vinegar to the skin helps to normalize its pH balance.

SORE FEET AND LEGS.

The next time you have sore, aching feet, fill the bathtub with several inches of warm water (enough to cover the feet). Add ½ cup of apple cider vinegar and walk back and forth in the solution for five minutes. Do this twice a day, and your feet and legs will feel relaxed.

SORE MUSCLES.

Soothe sore or tired muscles by wrapping them with a cloth dipped in apple cider vinegar. Leave the cloth on the area for five to ten minutes and repeat as often as needed. For even more relief, add a dash of cayenne to the vinegar.

LINIMENT FOR STIFF OR SORE MUSCLES.

Beat the yolk of one egg with two tablespoons of apple cider vinegar. Apply this mixture to the skin, rub in well, and allow to dry. Do this twice a day to relieve stiffness and soreness.

BATH FOR SORE MUSCLES.

To soothe sore muscles, add 2 cups of apple cider vinegar to your bathwater. It is great for sore muscles and fatigue, and it works better than expensive bath additives. Peppermint vinegar is especially effective.

Peppermint Vinegar Rub

> 1 pint vinegar
> 1 pint water
> 1 teaspoon peppermint oil

Mix together vinegar, water, and peppermint oil. This vinegar rub is ideal for soothing massages. Peppermint vinegar makes sore muscles feel better and adds a firmness to the texture of the skin.

SORE THROAT REMEDIES.

Here are some ways to relieve a sore throat.

Sore Throat Remedy 1

> ¼ cup honey
> ¼ cup apple cider vinegar

Mix together and take 1 tablespoon every 4 hours. This remedy is also recommended for the flu.

Sore Throat Remedy 2

Simply add 1 tablespoon of apple cider vinegar to a glass of warm water and gargle several times a day. This will ease the pain.

Sore Throat Remedy 3

½ cup apple cider vinegar
½ cup water
1 teaspoon cayenne
4 tablespoons honey

Mix together and take 3 tablespoons every 4 hours. This will ease the pain and speed healing.

SOUR STOMACH.
To make a sour stomach feel better, drink a glass of very warm water containing 1 teaspoon honey and 1 teaspoon vinegar.

STRESS RELIEF.
To relieve stress and leave you feeling energized, add a half pint of vinegar to a tub full of bathwater and soak for at least fifteen minutes. The skin will absorb some of the vinegar and the potassium in it, which will pep you up.

SUNBURN RELIEF.
To cool down a sunburn, rub full-strength vinegar (white or cider) on the skin. If you rub on vinegar before the sunburn starts, you will dramatically reduce the pain!

SWIMMER'S EAR PREVENTION.
See Earaches.

TOOTHACHE.
Rub apple cider vinegar on the tooth and surrounding gums for temporary relief from the pain.

ULCERS.
The idea that the acidity in apple cider vinegar can prevent ulcers may seem very odd to most people, but studies indicate that vinegar seems to cause the gastric system to secrete a chemical that actually protects the stomach and prevents ulcers.

VARICOSE VEINS.

Relieve and shrink varicose veins by wrapping the legs with a cloth wrung out with apple cider vinegar. Leave the vinegar-soaked cloth wrapped on your legs with them propped up for thirty minutes twice a day (morning and evening). Considerable relief will be noticed within six weeks. To speed up the healing process, follow each treatment with a glass of warm water with 1 teaspoon of apple cider vinegar added to it. If desired, add a teaspoon of honey to the mixture.

VOMITING.

See Nausea.

WEIGHT LOSS.

When dieting, drink a tonic of 2 cups warm water with 1 teaspoon of apple cider vinegar before each meal. It is said to help reduce the appetite and make the pounds come off more easily.

WINDBURN PROTECTION.

Protect skin from the chapping of windburn by applying a protective layer of olive oil and apple cider vinegar. Mix half olive oil and half apple cider vinegar. Rub a small amount on the face and other exposed skin areas.

■ Herbs for Home Remedies ■

Many herbs are known to remedy common health problems. Here are some of the more common herbs along with some spices and vegetables and what they can be used for. Steep the herb in white or distilled apple cider vinegar as you would tea, and use for the remedies listed. Do not use flavored vinegars derived from recipes in chapter 4, Making Vinegar at Home, because they are intended as food. When herb vinegars are used for medicinal purposes, the usual dose is 1 to 2 teaspoons added to a full glass of water. They can also be sprinkled onto salads or into meat or vegetable dishes. The very strong or bitter vinegars should be used sparingly and only for external purposes.

BAY:
Antiseptic; stimulates skin.

CHAMOMILE:
Antiseptic, astringent; cleans, softens, and soothes skin; highlights both dark and light hair.

CLOVE:
Stops vomiting. Clove vinegar usage dates back more than two thousand years. In China it was considered an aphrodisiac.

CLOVER, RED:
Soothes, heals.

COMFREY:
Astringent; heals and soothes burned skin; reduces swelling.

CUCUMBER:
Astringent; treatment for oily skin.

DANDELION:
Mild laxative, has anti-inflammatory effect on the intestines, works as a diuretic that is useful in lowering blood pressure.

ELDER FLOWERS:
Whitens, softens, heals, and cleanses skin. Helps relieve dry skin.

EUCALYPTUS:
Antiseptic; stimulates, soothes, and heals skin; and acts as a deodorant. Eucalyptus is the source of eucalyptol, which makes some cough drops so effective.

FENNEL:
Astringent; invigorates, cleanses, and smoothes skin.

HONEYSUCKLE:
Astringent; antiseptic.

JUNIPER:
Antiseptic; relieves sore muscles and joints; stimulates skin.

LAVENDER:
Antiseptic, treatment for oily skin; relieves joint pain, stimulates skin, relieves stressed nerves and headaches.

LEMON BALM:
Astringent; cleanses, smoothes, and soothes skin.

LEMON PEEL:
Treatment for oily skin, tonic, astringent; stimulates skin.

MARJORAM:
Antiseptic; relieves fatigue, sore throat, and aching muscles and joints; heals and soothes skin.

MINT:
Astringent; relieves headaches; refreshes, cools, heals, and stimulates skin.

ORANGE:
Treatment for dry skin; soothes skin.

OREGANO:
Antiseptic; relieves fatigue, sore throat, and aching muscles and joints; heels and soothes skin.

PARSLEY:
Adds shine to hair, lightens freckles and other skin blemishes, cleanses and conditions oily skin.

PEPPERMINT:
Like all other mints, peppermint soothes and calms the digestive system. Add a couple of teaspoons of peppermint vinegar to a glass of water to ease stomach pain, gas, or diarrhea.

ROSE:
Astringent; hydrates, heals, and soothes skin.

ROSEMARY:

Antiseptic, insect repellent; gives shine and body to hair, soothes and heals skin, stimulates and invigorates skin, relieves tension headaches, and eases dizziness.

SAGE:

Strong astringent for oily skin; stimulates skin, relieves aching muscles, conditions hair, and is a mild, natural tranquilizer for stress.

THYME:

Antiseptic; stimulates skin, deodorizes.

VIOLET:

Heals, soothes, and stimulates skin, clears skin blemishes.

WILLOW:

Astringent, disinfectant; helps relieve fever and chills, relieves muscle and joint pain.

MAKING
VINEGAR AT HOME

Making vinegar at home is a fun hobby that requires little in the way of money for supplies and equipment. Today you can find quite a variety of vinegars to buy, but making your own enables you to suit your own taste. Homemade vinegars are a treat to use in your own kitchen and also make wonderful gifts.

There are many different ways to make vinegar. It is not a complicated process although your supplies need to be kept clean and sanitized throughout the vinegar-making process. If you are making vinegar from a food product instead of wine, wash and clean the food product thoroughly. Clean the utensils and bowls or other equipment with soap and water and sanitize them by rinsing with almost boiling water or run them through the dishwasher. Use plastic or wooden spoons, a plastic strainer or colander, glass or plastic measuring cups, and glass or enamel pots and pans. One of the most basic rules for making or flavoring vinegar is to avoid letting the vinegar make contact with certain metals such as aluminum. Since vinegar is such an acidic substance, it will leach the metal molecules from a metal pot, bowl, or spoon. Be certain to use only glass or plastic bottles for storing and aging vinegars. Make sure that you have tight-fitting lids or corks for bottles to keep out any unwanted pests that like the smell and flavor of your vinegar. If the jar in which you store vinegar has a metal lid, place a double thickness of plastic wrap over the mouth of the jar to keep the metal lid from touching the vinegar.

■ Bottles for Homemade Vinegars or ■ Herb and Flavored Vinegars

You can buy bottles for vinegars at most houseware stores, but you don't have to spend a fortune on fancy ones for your home-made vinegars. A container for vinegar can be any type of bottle as long as it is not made of metal. Metal lids can be used if they are wrapped in a double thickness of plastic wrap to keep the metal lid from touching the vinegar. Glass bottles or jars, special decanters with plastic lids, rubber rings, glass tops, or corks are all fine for storing vinegars (make sure they have been properly scrubbed and sterilized with boiling water). Bottles that once held clear beer, wine cooler, water, ketchup, or barbecue sauce all make nice vinegar bottles.

Make your homemade vinegars look special by adding a cork to the top. You can buy corks at craft stores or a wine-and-beer-making supply store. For an elegant touch, finish the bottle by dipping the cork and bottle top into wax. Use a mixture of half paraffin and half beeswax for easy opening later. Tie a ribbon around the bottle and add a favorite recipe that includes the vinegar, and you have a pleasing, inexpensive gift.

■ The Main Ingredient ■

Vinegar can be made at home from any fruit or vegetable matter that contains sugar or has enough convertible starch to provide sugar for fermentation. Grapes produce some of the most popular vinegars, but there are many other fruits and some berries that make exceptional vinegars. Raspberry vinegar is very popular for its outstanding taste and aroma. Apple cider vinegar is common and used for many things including cooking, cleaning, and maintaining good health. You can make special gourmet vinegars from cherries, peaches, pineapples, oranges, or any other fruit you like. When you make your own vinegar, there are no limitations. You can experiment with different flavors and come up with your own specialty vinegars.

▪ A Simple Process ▪

Making vinegar at home is simple. No expensive equipment is required. All you need to make wine vinegar is a clean jug, a little unpasteurized vinegar, a piece of cheesecloth, and a bottle of wine. Your homemade wine vinegar will taste better than anything you can buy at the grocery store if you start with a good quality wine. You also will have the satisfaction of knowing that no wine will be wasted around your house; instead, it will be turned into vinegar.

Acetobacter is the genus of bacteria that turns wine or any other alcoholic liquid into vinegar. These bacteria float freely in the air and settle into any open container of wine and go straight to work without any special coaxing. Basically they eat alcohol and turn it into acetic acid. This process requires oxygen, so place the container of wine in a location that gets plenty of fresh air. The working bacteria will start to form a whitish-colored veil, called mother or mother of vinegar, on the surface of the liquid.

Temperature is also a factor when making wine vinegar. Acetobacters are not fond of extreme temperatures. They work slowly in temperatures below 70 degrees Fahrenheit, and they also become less active at temperatures above 90 degrees.

MAKING MOTHER.
When making wine vinegar, you can speed up the process by adding some mother of vinegar from another batch. If you don't

have a batch of vinegar to use, you can make some mother of vinegar to speed up the process. Place two tablespoons of unpasteurized and unfiltered vinegar and 8 ounces of wine or cider in a bowl; leave the mixture in a warm, sunny windowsill for two weeks, during which a skin will have formed on top of the mixture. This is the *Acetobacter* bacteria, or mother, that is needed to speed the process of turning wine and other alcohols into vinegar.

Skim off the mother and transfer it with 8 ounces of the same type of alcohol to a widemouthed container or bowl. Cover the top with cheesecloth or with a thin dish towel to keep bugs and dust out of the liquid while allowing the liquid to get a good supply of oxygen. Leave the container in a warm place for one month. Skim off the mother and transfer it with 8 ounces of the same type of alcohol to make another batch of vinegar. Then strain the vinegar through a double thickness of cheesecloth. You can continue this process as long as you add fresh alcohol to the mother each time. Pour the vinegar into a bottle, and it's ready when you need it.

Use your homemade vinegar just as you would a bottle bought from the store. If you want to add flavors to your homemade vinegar, steep the ingredient of your choice into the vinegar as soon as you have strained it. (See Flavored-Vinegar Recipes below for more directions and ideas.) You can use your homemade vinegars for most of the recipes. When making pickles or canning vegetables, however, a commercial vinegar with a standard amount of acidity is necessary. (Vinegar must have at least 4 to 6 percent acidity to keep pickles from spoiling. Homemade vinegar is more or less acidic than a standard commercial vinegar.)

■ Homemade Apple-Cider Vinegar ■

First make a tart apple cider. Combine several types of apples. You'll want some sweet apples and some tart ones; you can even add some crab apples. The more sweet apples you include the stronger your vinegar will be because the high sugar content of sweet apples produces more alcohol, which changes into acid. The more tart apples you use, the sharper the flavor will be. Experiment with your mix and add more sweet or tart apples depending on your taste.

To make the cider, chop 12 large apples (there is no need to peel them), and when they turn brown, crush them in a cider press or press them through a kitchen strainer. Collect the cider in a glass container. Never try to make vinegar with store-bought apple cider because it contains preservatives and may have been pasteurized, so it will not ferment properly. Occasionally you can buy organic, unpasteurized cider from a local apple farm. If you buy cider from a local farm, ask the farmer if the cider is simply pressed apples to make sure it has not been pasteurized and that no preservatives have been added. In general, local farms make cider only on the weekends when customers are plentiful, because without pasteurization, cider has a very short shelf life.

Pour the cider (you'll have about 2 to 3 cups) into a clean plastic milk container and cap it with a small balloon. The balloon will expand as carbon dioxide is released, while keeping air away from the cider. When all the sugar has converted to alcohol, it becomes hard cider. This will take about one to six weeks, depending on the sugar content of the apples and the temperature. Taste the cider after one week to determine if it is ready. If it is not ready, put the balloon back on the top and leave it for another week. Continue this process until it has turned to hard cider.

You don't need to add yeast to make apple cider vinegar, since wild yeast exists on apple surfaces and in the air. If a gray foam forms on the top of the cider, it is excess yeast. This is harmless; skim it off the top and discard it.

Next, pour the hard cider into a wide crock or glass bowl, so a much larger surface is exposed to air than when it was in the milk jug. Put a thin cloth over the crock or bowl to keep dust and bugs out while allowing air to circulate. In about two months you will have created apple cider vinegar. Wild spores floating in the air will eventually make your hard cider ferment into vinegar. To speed up the process, you can add mother to the cider. Simply smear a slice of toast with mother and lay it gently on the surface of the cider. By adding the mother you can expect your apple cider vinegar to be ready in about one month.

Try to keep your vinegar in progress at a temperature close to 80 degrees. If the temperature is much hotter, the bacteria needed for fermenting will be killed. If the temperature drops too low, the wild spores will become dormant.

EASY APPLE-CIDER VINEGAR

Place 12 large cut-up apples (no need to peel or core apples, just wash them) in a crock or glass bowl and cover them with warm tap water. Cover the bowl with a thin cloth and keep the mixture in a warm place for 4 to 6 months. To reduce the time to 2 to 3 months, you can add a piece of raw bread dough to the mixture. The added yeast from the bread dough helps to speed up the process. Strain off the liquid. Let this sweet apple cider stand open in a jug for 5 to 6 weeks, and it will turn into vinegar.

EASY HOMEMADE-WINE VINEGAR

Here's an easy method for making wine vinegar. Mash two pounds of raisins by simply placing them in a large bowl and mashing them with a potato masher or the back of a fork. Basically, you want to break open the skin of the raisins so the juice will mix with the water. Add to a gallon of soft water in a 2-gallon crock or a large glass bowl. Cover the top with a thin cloth to keep out bugs and dust. (Use a rubber band to hold the cloth over the top.) Let the bowl stand in a warm place, and in about 2 months the liquid will become white wine vinegar. Strain the liquid into an attractive glass and discard the pulpy residue.

THRIFTY CIDER VINEGAR

Here's a way to make use of fruit scraps—the peelings and even the cores!

Place apple and peach peelings and a few crushed grapes or grape skins in a widemouthed jar, crock, or glass bowl. Cover the peels with cold water. Set in a warm place and add a couple of fresh apple cores and peelings every few days. When a scum forms on top, stop adding fruit and let the mixture thicken for a couple of weeks. Then let the mixture sit for one month before tasting to see if it has turned to vinegar. When vinegar is strong enough to suit your taste, strain it through a double layer of cheesecloth.

EASY WINE CONVERSION

To convert wine into vinegar, leave the wine bottle open with a thin cloth covering the top. During warm summer months you can place the bottle in direct sunlight, and you'll have a supply of vinegar in about 2 weeks. During the winter, you can leave the open bottle in the house, and in about one month the wine will turn to vinegar.

QUICK WINE CONVERSION

If you want to turn red or white wine into wine vinegar in about half the time, you can do so by adding some mother of vinegar to the wine. Pour the wine into a jar or bowl and add a little actively fermenting wine vinegar (not distilled vinegar) to it. (An actively fermenting vinegar has a slight sediment—the mother—on the bottom of the bottle.) Cover the jar with cheesecloth or a thin dish towel and use a rubber band to hold it in place. Fermentation will take place only if there's plenty of oxygen present. You will have a new supply of wine vinegar in just a few weeks.

HONEY VINEGAR

You can make a rich-tasting honey vinegar by pouring 8 cups of boiling water over 2½ pounds of honey. Stir until the honey is melted. In a separate bowl, dissolve 1 package (or cake) of yeast in 1 tablespoon of warm water. Let it sit for 15 minutes, until it is frothy. Spread the active yeast on a slice of toast and float it (yeast side up) on the top of the honey water. Cover the container with a thin cloth and let it sit for 3 weeks. Take out the piece of bread, skim the scum off the top, and strain the liquid, discarding all but the strained liquid. Let the strained liquid stand for 30 to 40 days, until it turns into vinegar.

NOTE: Dark or strong-flavored honeys will ferment much faster than light, mild-flavored ones. Add a cup of fruit juice or ½ cup molasses to light honey to speed up the process.

■ The Orleans Method of Vinegar Making ■

Many people who make homemade vinegar on a regular basis follow this method, which is not complicated once you get set up. You'll need to buy or make what is called a converter. The converter is a container in which the wine turns into vinegar. It can be a small wooden barrel (oak or chestnut are the preferred woods) that holds about 2 to 4 quarts of liquid, a specially made crock, or a food-grade-quality plastic jug. The converter must have a spigot at the bottom for draining out fresh vinegar and a hole at the top for adding new wine to the mixture. It also needs a few holes placed in a horizontal row about two-thirds of the way up the container. The holes must be covered with mesh screening to keep flies and bugs out of the brew.

To start making vinegar, pour 2 cups of wine into your vinegar converter. Add 4 cups unpasteurized vinegar. An unpasteurized vinegar is sometimes called an active vinegar because it contains living (active) acetobacters. If you cannot find unpasteurized vinegar (health foods stores usually carry it), add the same amount of vinegar and a piece of mother to the mixture (see Making Mother, page 96). Save a mother from a previous batch or borrow a piece from a friend who makes vinegar. You can also buy mother of vinegar from stores that sell vinegar-making supplies. (See page 189, Mail Order Resources.)

The vinegar helps protect the wine from attack by undesirable microorganisms, and the mother of vinegar speeds up the process. When adding mother of vinegar to the mixture you need not worry about matching the color of vinegars. For instance, you can use the mother of vinegar from a red wine vinegar to make a white wine vinegar. The white wine vinegar may have a very slight blush to it, but it will not affect the taste.

After one week, pour 2 cups of wine into the mixture and continue to add wine at weekly intervals until the converter is filled to just below the row of air vents. As you add the wine, it is very important not to disturb the surface of the vinegar. To prevent disturbing the surface, fit a hole in the top of the converter with a funnel that has a very long neck. The neck needs to reach deep inside the converter and as close to the bottom as possible. Pour the additional wine slowly through the funnel. If you cannot find a funnel with a long enough neck, use a piece of glass tubing to reach inside the converter and attach a funnel to the top of the glass tubing.

As the mother starts to grow, it will look like small grease spots on the top of the liquid. They will spread, eventually becoming a grayish or whitish veil. The mother must get oxygen to do its work. If you pour new wine into the converter, it can splash and may cause the veil to sink. It will then no longer be in contact with oxygen and the mother will stop working. Over time, the mother will multiply and the veil will become thicker. It may get so thick that it will sink due to the weight. If this happens, a new layer will quickly form. Some vinegar makers say that a sunken mother will add an off taste to the vinegar. When the mother sinks from its own weight, it is a good time to remove the ingredients from the converter; wash it clean and start the process over with fresh wine and unpasteurized vinegar.

After about a month in the converter, you can start tasting the vinegar by pouring a little out from the spigot. Once your vinegar tastes as strong as you like it, pour it through a coffee filter into a bottle. Fill it to the top and cork it. (Do not use metal caps for vinegar containers. If you can't find any other type cap, line the metal cap with several layers of plastic wrap.) Add the same amount of new wine to the converter. For example, if you bottled 8 ounces of vinegar from the converter, add 8 ounces of wine to the mixture.

Once the bottle of vinegar is filled and closed it will be protected from oxygen and the acetobacters will stop working. You can pasteurize your vinegar to protect it from any further changes. All you have to do is heat it to a minimum of 140 degrees Fahrenheit in an open, nonreactive container. Keep the temperature of the vinegar at 140 degrees but no higher than 160 degrees for twenty minutes. Then pour the vinegar into sterilized bottles and seal with nonmetallic stoppers. This process will drive off some of the delicate flavors of the vinegar. Most vinegar lovers draw off only as much vinegar from the converter as they can use within about a month and skip the pasteurization process.

If your vinegar tastes too strong for your liking, you can add water until you reach the balance that works for you. Testing your vinegar for its exact strength is not absolutely necessary unless you plan to use it for pickling. Let your tastebuds be your guide. When you need to know the strength of a vinegar in applications such as pickling and preserving, use a commercial vinegar instead of a homemade one.

Don't forget to keep "feeding" your vinegar converter. Vinegar is a living product, and to keep the vinegar healthy and thriving, you need to add fresh wine at least once a month.

CHECKING THE STRENGTH OF
HOMEMADE VINEGAR

The acid content of store-bought vinegar is standardized at 5 percent, but homemade vinegars can vary. If you like to know the strength of your concoction, here is one way to determine the percent of acid in a batch of homemade vinegar.

> ½ cup water
> 2 teaspoons baking soda
> ¼ cup of the water in which a head of red cabbage was cooked
> commercial vinegar

1. Mix the water and baking soda together in a glass.
2. Into two other clear glasses, pour soda water.
3. Add ⅛ cup cabbage water to each glass of plain water.
4. Use a glass or plastic dropper to put 7 drops of commercial vinegar into one glass of the cabbage water.
5. Rinse the dropper.
6. Put 20 drops of the soda water into the same glass and stir well (use a plastic spoon, not metal). The water will turn blue.
7. Now mix 7 drops of your vinegar into the second glass of the cabbage-flavored water.
8. Rinse the dropper.
9. Add soda water to the glass containing your vinegar and cabbage water, one drop at a time. Stir after each drop. Count the drops.
10. When the color of your homemade vinegar water turns the same shade of blue as the commercial vinegar water, the acid content of the two glasses is equal.

To find the percent of acid in your homemade vinegar, divide the number of drops of soda water you added to it by 4. For example, if you added 20 drops of soda water to your vinegar, divide by 4; the acid content is 5 percent (the same as most commercial vinegars). The more soda water it takes to make your vinegar match the color of the commercial vinegar, the stronger your homemade vinegar is.

■ Flavored-Vinegar Recipes ■

Making flavored vinegars is a fun way to perk up your favorite recipes without adding extra fat or calories. In the following recipes use distilled apple cider vinegar unless otherwise instructed.

You don't have to buy special bottles to store your flavored vinegars in. Instead, save bottles that once held wine, honey, water, wine cooler, or soda. Wash the bottles in very hot, soapy water or sterilize them in the dishwasher before using. Don't let a metal lid come into contact with your vinegar; buy some corks at a craft store to close the bottles. If you cannot find a cork to fit one of your bottles, cover the inside of the metal lid with several thicknesses of plastic wrap to keep the metal from coming into contact with the vinegar.

When making herbed vinegar, heat the vinegar to hot (but not boiling) before you pour it over the herbs. This will speed up the process and make the vinegar more flavorful. Always use a nonreactive pan when heating vinegar. I prefer to avoid using metal of any type when working with vinegar. Stick with glass or enamel pots and pans and plastic or wood utensils to ensure the best quality of your flavored vinegars and of the recipes that include vinegar.

Herbal and flavored vinegars can be used in any recipe calling for vinegar. The flavor will increase the complexity of the dish. With a little experimentation, you'll find which flavors add the most to your recipes.

SHELF LIFE OF FLAVORED VINEGARS
Herb and flavored vinegars will keep about two years, and possibly longer, if stored in a cool dark place. Some fruit vinegars

such as raspberry, blueberry, and strawberry tend to caramelize after a while. This process causes the vinegar to turn slightly brown, which is not as pretty as the original clear red or violet vinegar. Try to use these vinegars up in two to three months to avoid this discoloration. Vinegar has a high acid content, and it is used as a preservative itself, so spoiling is never a problem.

EQUIVALENT LIQUID MEASURES

3 teaspoons = 1 tablespoon
2 tablespoons = 1 ounce
5⅓ tablespoons = ⅓ cup
8 ounces = 1 cup
16 tablespoons = 1 cup
2 cups = 1 pint
16 ounces = 1 pint
2 pints = 1 quart
32 ounces = 1 quart
4 quarts = 1 gallon

BASIC RECIPE FOR BERRY VINEGARS

1 to 1½ pounds of ripe berries, washed and drained (see list on page 107)
1 quart white vinegar

In a large glass bowl, prepare berries as indicated below. Stir in the vinegar. Pour into a large jar for aging. Cover the jar with plastic wrap and secure the wrap on top with a rubber band. Let age in a cool, dark place for about 3 to 4 weeks, then strain through a cheesecloth-lined plastic strainer until clear. Pour into bottles and seal.

Makes about 1 quart.

Any of the following berries may be used in the Basic Recipe:

- Blackberries: 1 pound crushed well
- Blueberries: 1 pound, ground in a blender with ⅓ cup of the vinegar
- Cranberries: 1 pound, ground in a blender with ⅓ cup of the vinegar
- Currants: 1 pound, ground in a blender with ⅓ cup of the vinegar
- Raspberries: 1 to 1½ pounds, crushed well
- Strawberries: 1 pound, hulled and crushed well

QUICK AND EASY JAM VINEGAR

You can easily make fruit-flavored vinegars by adding preserves or jams to a jar of red or white wine vinegar. Add 2 tablespoons of preserves or jam to 1 cup of vinegar. Simply let it stand for about a week. You can use the fruit-flavored vinegar in salad dressings or add a little cream to it to make a delicious sauce for meat or poultry.

FRUIT-VINEGAR SELTZER

Strawberry and raspberry vinegars make particularly delicious flavored drinks.

2 tablespoons fruit vinegar
8 ounces of seltzer or lemon-lime soda

Mix the fruit vinegar into the seltzer or lemon-lime soda and enjoy a nice tangy drink.

BASIC RECIPE FOR FRUIT VINEGARS

1 to 2 pounds ripe fruit; washed and drained (see list
below)
1 quart white or red wine vinegar

In a large glass bowl, prepare fruit as indicated below. Stir in
the vinegar. Pour into a large jar for aging. Cover the jar with a
dish towel and secure the towel on top with a rubber band. Let
age in a cool, dark place for at least one month, then strain
through a cheesecloth and plastic strainer until clear. Pour into
bottles and seal.

Makes about 1 quart.

Any of the following fruits may be used in the Basic Recipe:

- Cherries: 1 pound cherries, pitted and ground in a
  blender with ⅓ cup of the vinegar
- Kiwi: 9 kiwifruit, peeled and finely chopped
- Lemon, Lime, or Orange: 3 of any fruit; remove the peel
  and the white layer; squeeze the fruit and pulp into the
  vinegar. Note: When bottling, add a few fresh spirals of
  peel to each bottle for color.
- Peach: 1 pound peaches, peeled, pitted, and chopped into
  bits
- Pear: 1 pound pears, peeled, pitted, and chopped into bits
- Pineapple: ½ fresh pineapple; remove peel, discard; finely
  chop fruit. Add any juice to vinegar when mixing.
- Rhubarb: 1 pound rhubarb, finely chopped. In a
  saucepan heat the rhubarb with ¼ cup water until it
  comes to a boil. Cool to room temperature before contin-
  uing.
- Watermelon: about 3 pounds. Remove skin and green
  rind. Save the rind to make Watermelon Rind Pickles.
  (See page 142.) Mash remaining watermelon meat with a

fork. Don't worry about removing the seeds, they add color to the bottled vinegar.

Makes 1 quart.

BASIC RECIPE FOR HERB VINEGARS

Use any fresh herb, blossom and all. If you like, you can combine several herbs for unique flavors. Experiment with your favorites. Tarragon and thyme work well together. Chives and parsley, rosemary and mint, or oregano and basil are also excellent herb combinations.

handful of the fresh herbs of your choice
2 cups cider vinegar
2 cups white vinegar
1 tablespoon granulated sugar

Wash the herbs and place several sprigs in each sterilized bottle. Bring the vinegars and sugar to a boil in a large saucepan and pour over the herbs. Cork tightly. Store at room temperature away from direct sunlight. Refrigerate after opening. Let the herb vinegar age for 2 weeks before using.

Makes 1 quart.

BASIC RECIPE FOR SPICE VINEGAR

1 quart vinegar
dried spices (see list on page 110)

Gently heat the vinegar in a stainless steel pot on the stovetop or in a large glass bowl in the microwave. Add the spices to the hot vinegar. Cool and strain until you have a clear vinegar. Bottle and label. It is ready to use immediately; no aging time is necessary with this method.

Makes 1 quart.

You can use any one of the following spices or mix two of them for a unique flavor.

- 2 tablespoons whole anise seeds
- 2 cinnamon sticks
- 2 tablespoons whole cloves
- 3 tablespoons peppercorns

NOTE: Add a few whole spices to each finished bottle for decoration.

BASIC RECIPE FOR VEGETABLE VINEGAR

1 quart white or red wine vinegar
ripe vegetables (see list below)
Use any one of the following:
- *6 garlic cloves, peeled and mashed flat*
- *3 bunches of green onions, sliced thin*
- *1 pound peppers (green, red, or yellow), seeded and chopped*
- *4 hot peppers, seeded and sliced thin*
- *1 pound sweet onions, peeled and sliced*

Prepare the vegetables as directed and mix them with the vinegar. Store in covered jars to age for at least one month. Remove vegetables by straining through cheesecloth until clear, then bottle. Note: Add several pieces of fresh vegetables, such as onion or pepper rings or garlic cloves, to the final bottles.

Makes 1 quart.

BASIC RECIPE FOR FLOWER VINEGAR

Always use flowers that have not been treated for insects, mold, or fungus. And be certain to use only edible flowers or leaves. Nasturtium vinegar is very popular (see the recipe on page 111).

Other interesting flowers that you can use include roses, violets, and herb flowers like chive blossoms.

> *1 quart cider vinegar or white vinegar*
> *¼ to ½ cup flower petals, thoroughly washed and drained*

Combine the vinegar and petals in a large glass jar and cover tightly. Age 3 to 4 months, then strain and use.

Makes 1 quart.

NASTURTIUM VINEGAR

> *1 quart freshly picked nasturtium flowers*
> *2 cloves*
> *1 clove garlic, minced*
> *6 peppercorns*
> *1 large onion, finely chopped*
> *1 quart vinegar*

Pick through the flowers to remove any dead or damaged flowers, rinse gently, and pat dry. Combine all the ingredients and let age for 6 weeks. Strain and use.

Makes 1 quart.

SPICY HERB VINEGAR

The herb and spice combinations for this recipe are limited only by your imagination.

> *1 generous handful of your favorite fresh herb, finely*
>   *chopped*
> *1 quart apple cider vinegar*
> *1 tablespoon of your favorite dried whole spice, such*
>   *as allspice, cinnamon stick, cloves, or grated fresh*
>   *gingerroot*

Mix the chopped herb with the vinegar and spices in a large glass jar and cover tightly. Age for 4 weeks. Strain through a double layer of cheesecloth until the liquid is clear, then bottle and label. Add fresh sprigs of herbs or whole spices to the final bottles.

Makes 1 quart.

CHIVE BLOSSOM AND DILL VINEGAR

2 cups chive blossoms
2 cups fresh dill sprigs
2 quarts vinegar
black peppercorns
chive blossoms
8 fresh dill flowers, if available

In a clean glass bottle or jar, place the chive blossoms, dill sprigs, and vinegar. Cover the bottle with a tight-fitting top and let the mixture steep for 2 weeks.

At the end of the steeping time, strain the vinegar into eight clean 8-ounce bottles. Add 8 to 10 peppercorns, 2 to 3 chive blossoms, and 1 fresh dill flower to each bottle. Seal the bottles with tight-fitting tops or corks. Keep refrigerated.

Makes eight 8-ounce bottles.

HOT PEPPER VINEGAR

12 to 15 long, thin fresh hot red peppers, washed and
*   pierced with a needle*
2 parsley sprigs
white wine vinegar

In a clean 8- to 10-ounce bottle, pack the peppers and parsley. Fill the bottle with enough white wine vinegar to cover the peppers completely. Cover the bottle with a tight-fitting top and let the mixture steep for one week. As the vinegar is used, replace with enough vinegar to completely cover the peppers. Keep refrigerated.

Makes one 8- to 10-ounce bottle.

MINT VINEGAR

Stuff an empty bottle full of fresh mint leaves. Fill the bottle with hot (not boiling) vinegar. Cap and age for at lest 6 weeks. Strain and use with lamb or add to drinks.

ROSE PETAL AND THYME VINEGAR

2 cups loosely packed rose petals (be sure to use roses that have not been chemically treated)
1 large bunch thyme
2 quarts vinegar
black peppercorns
rosebuds
sprigs of fresh thyme

In a clean glass bottle or jar, place the rose petals, thyme, and vinegar. Cover the bottle with a tight-fitting lid and let mixture steep for one week.

At the end of steeping time, strain the vinegar into eight clean 8-ounce bottles. Add 8 to 10 peppercorns, 1 or 2 rosebuds, and 1 or 2 sprigs of thyme to each bottle. Herbs should be completely covered with vinegar. Seal bottles with tight-fitting lids or corks. Keep refrigerated.

Makes eight 8-ounce bottles.

SUPREME VINEGAR

This old-fashioned recipe can be used for a light salad dressing, and it makes a wonderful seasoning for gravies, sauces, and stews.

> *2 teaspoons allspice*
> *1 teaspoon whole black peppercorns*
> *1 tablespoon nutmeg*
> *2 tablespoons horseradish*
> *pinch of cayenne*
> *1 tablespoon salt*
> *1 tablespoon sugar*
> *4 cups vinegar*

Crush the allspice and peppercorns with a wooden mallet. Place all ingredients except the vinegar into a large saucepan. Pour the vinegar on top and bring to a boil. Remove from the heat, pour into a covered container, and let stand for at least 2 weeks. Strain through a double thickness of cheesecloth and bottle in clean containers. Keep refrigerated.

Makes 1 quart.

LEMON-DILL VINEGAR

This vinegar is perfect in marinades for fish or in dressing for seafood or tossed salads.

> *1 lemon*
> *4 to 5 fresh dill sprigs*
> *1 cup distilled white vinegar*

Remove the lemon peel in a thin spiral. Squeeze out the lemon juice into a clean jar. Add the lemon peel and dill sprigs. Heat the vinegar to just below the boiling point. Pour the hot vinegar over the lemon and dill. Cap tightly. Allow to stand 3 to 4 weeks. Strain the vinegar, discarding the peel and dill. Pour the clear vinegar into a clean bottle adding a fresh lemon peel and dill sprig for garnish. Seal tightly.

Makes 8 ounces.

THREE-ONION VINEGAR

Three-onion vinegar is perfect to use in dressings for salad or slaw.

> *4 cups vinegar*
> *1 large red onion, finely chopped*
> *6 large scallions, finely chopped*
> *8 large garlic cloves, cut in slivers*

Bring the vinegar to a boil. Place the onion, scallions, and garlic in a 2-quart nonreactive bowl or glass measure. Add the boiling vinegar. Let cool to room temperature, then cover with plastic wrap and let steep at least 3 days. Strain through a cheesecloth-lined or coffee-filter-lined strainer into a clean 1-quart bottle.

Makes 1 quart.

HORSERADISH VINEGAR

> *1 quart vinegar*
> *¼ cup freshly grated horseradish*

In a nonreactive saucepan, bring the vinegar to a boil. Add the horseradish and transfer to a clean glass container. Seal the container and set it aside for 3 to 4 days. Strain out the grated horseradish until you are left with clear vinegar.

Makes 1 quart.

SAGE CRANBERRY-APPLE VINEGAR

This makes a very pretty pink-colored vinegar. Perfect for holiday gift giving.

> *4 cups vinegar*
> *3 tablespoons sugar*
> *peel from one apple (remove with a vegetable peeler)*
> *3 large sprigs fresh sage*
> *¼ cup fresh cranberries*
> *2 wooden skewers*
> *1 quart bottle*

In a medium nonreactive saucepan, combine the vinegar and sugar; heat until simmering over medium heat (do not boil), stirring to dissolve the sugar. Roll up the apple peel pieces and insert into a clean 1-quart bottle. Add the sage sprigs. Place cranberries on the wooden skewers and insert into the bottle. (Cut the wooden skewers if necessary to fit them in the bottle.) Fill the bottle with the hot vinegar mixture. Let it cool before corking or sealing the bottle. Let the vinegar stand for at least 2 weeks.

Makes 1 quart.

TARRAGON VINEGAR

Tarragon vinegar tastes wonderful on cooked and raw vegetables.

> *¼ cup tarragon leaves*
> *1 pint vinegar*

Put the tarragon leaves in a pint bottle and add vinegar. Let the vinegar age for 8 weeks before straining and using.

Makes 1 pint.

IMMEDIATE-USE HERB OR FLAVORED VINEGAR

Use this recipe to make flavored vinegar you can use immediately. No waiting for the herbs or fruits to flavor the vinegar; in this recipe the flavor transfers to the vinegar immediately.

With this recipe you may end up with a strong-flavored vinegar. You can either use sparingly or thin down the flavor with more apple cider vinegar. It's always best to start with too much flavor instead of not enough. This is a quick and easy way to make use of excess herbs.

> *1 cup fresh green herb leaves packed tightly (Herbs such as mint, sage, chives, oregano, basil, lavender flowers and leaves, and rosemary are just a few of my favorites for this recipe.)*
> *1 cup apple cider vinegar*
> *pinch of salt*

Put the herbs, vinegar, and salt into a blender and blend on high speed for 30 seconds. Strain through a single layer of cheesecloth or a fine metal strainer into a clean glass bottle. Press on the solids when straining to extract all the vinegar and the flavor. If possible, use the vinegar immediately while it is a delicate green color. The color changes quickly from the pretty green to a brownish color. (The flavor will not change when it turns to brown, it is just not as pretty to look at.) Store the vinegar in a cool, dark place covered tightly with a nonmetallic lid. Add a fresh leaf or two to the final product for easy identification.

NOTE: You can use fresh herbs, vegetables, or flowers for this recipe. Just be sure the items you choose have not been sprayed with any insecticides. Experiment with your favorite flavors and tastes.

Makes about 1 cup.

BROWN GRAVY VINEGAR

Add 2 tablespoons of this vinegar to meat gravy or stews to add flavor and make the gravy a nice color.

1 quart vinegar
1 onion, grated
3 red peppers, finely chopped
2 tablespoons dark brown sugar
1 tablespoon celery seed
1 tablespoon dry mustard
1 teaspoon black pepper
½ teaspoon salt

Stir all ingredients into a quart of vinegar. Let age for 3 to 4 weeks.

Makes 1 quart.

COOKING WITH VINEGAR

Vinegar has long been the "secret ingredient" in many of the best recipes. It has been used to enhance, preserve, and flavor foods for thousands of years. Vinegar brings out the natural flavor of foods without adding fat. Just a touch of vinegar in some of your recipes can turn them from plain to gourmet. Vinegar adds a zippy flavor to meat, fish, sauces, stews, and vegetable dishes. When a sauce lacks flavor, add a dash of vinegar instead of reaching for the salt shaker. Vinegar is the perfect flavoring choice for people watching their weight or cholesterol intake (and who isn't these days!).

Vinegars will keep almost indefinitely if left unopened in a dark, cool place. Vinegars, like fine wines, improve with age. Once opened, most vinegars will retain their flavor for at least three to four months, and cider vinegar will keep for about six months. The vinegar won't go bad after this time, but it will continue to lose flavor. Keep bottles of vinegar tightly sealed after opening.

Types of Vinegars

Making homemade vinegar is a fun and easy hobby (see page 94 for more information). Of course, many commercial varieties of vinegar are available from the grocery store for a reasonable price.

DISTILLED WHITE VINEGAR (also called white vinegar) is made from grain alcohol and is used as a flavoring, especially in salad dressings and as a pickling solution. It can be whisked with oil and herbs to make a dressing for steamed vegetables or fish. Distilled vinegar is virtually free of fat, sodium, calories, and cholesterol. Although distilled vinegar tends to have the harshest flavor, it is the most popular and most often used vinegar, not for its cooking value, but for its use in household cleaning.

CIDER VINEGAR is made from apples and is probably the most common cooking vinegar in the house. It has a tart flavor and a caramel color. It adds flavor to foods without adding sodium, fat, calories, or cholesterol. Sprinkle a few drops of plain cider vinegar on lightly steamed green beans, asparagus, broccoli, cauliflower, brussels sprouts, cabbage, or other fresh foods to enhance the flavor. Cider vinegar is also nice on smoked meat or on fish and on strong-tasting lettuces. The fruit flavor of the vinegar intensifies when used in cooked dishes, which makes cider vinegar a perfect choice for sautéed fruits. Cider vinegar is second only to distilled white vinegar in availability.

MALT VINEGAR is made from ale and is most often served with fish and chips. It is slightly sweeter than distilled vinegar. Malt vinegar is a good choice for salad dressings.

CANE VINEGAR is made from fermented sugarcane extract and water. Cane vinegar has a low acidity (about 4 percent) and is used most often in Philippine cooking. You can usually find cane vinegar in ethnic grocery stores or in health food stores.

RICE VINEGAR is made in Japan and China. It is a white vinegar that has a sharp, clean taste. Many people feel that rice vinegar has a more mellow taste than that of distilled white vinegar.

WINE VINEGAR is made from fermented red and white wines, sherry, or champagne. Wine vinegars have the mildest flavors and are the most versatile for cooking. They are typically used for salad dressings, sauces, and marinades. Sherry vinegars are less acidic than other wine vinegars. Like fine wines, wine and sherry vinegars are frequently aged in wooden casks or barrels to ensure a smooth taste.

BALSAMIC VINEGAR is made from the unfermented juice of the white Trebbiano grape. These grapes are unique to the area around Modena, Italy. The Trebbiano grape juice is boiled down to a sweet and very fruity syrup that is then aged in wooden barrels. The finished vinegar must be aged at least six years before it is sold. It is not uncommon to find balsamic vinegar that is fifty to a hundred years old; but just like vintage wine, the price increases with the number of years it has been aged. Balsamic vinegar is very popular for its intense flavor.

HERB VINEGARS are good-quality wine or cider vinegars that have been flavored (infused) with herbs. There are many different herb vinegars available such as basil, mint, rosemary, dill, chive, tarragon, and oregano. You can easily make your own herb vinegars with your favorite flavors for a fraction of the price of prepared vinegars. (See Flavored-Vinegar Recipes on page 105 for directions.) Herb vinegars add a burst of flavor to ordinary foods. A plain chicken breast can be made into a special treat with just a splash of herb vinegar.

FRUIT VINEGARS are made with good-quality wine or cider vinegars and a variety of fruits such as strawberry, peach, cranberry, lemon, orange, or kiwifruit. Fruit vinegars add flavor to fruit salads, salad dressings, or meats. Fruit vinegars are easy to make at home with fresh seasonal fruit. Fruit vinegars are some of the most flavorful and beautiful vinegars. (See Flavored-Vinegar Recipes on page 105 for directions and ideas.)

OTHER VINEGARS may include those made from mead, potatoes, cashew nuts, molasses, coconuts, pineapple, and any fermented liquor.

▪ Hints for Cooking with Vinegar ▪

Try some of these vinegar cooking tips, and you'll find more ways to use vinegar with each meal. Use inexpensive white distilled vinegar or distilled apple cider vinegar unless the tip calls for something different. In recipes, homemade vinegar or more expensive vinegars are better because they add more flavor. For household hints (rather than recipes), cheaper vinegar works equally well.

RED WINE VINEGAR SUBSTITUTE.
When a recipe calls for red wine vinegar and you don't have any on hand, simply mix 2 parts vinegar with 1 part dry red wine to make a substitute for the amount of red wine vinegar called for in the recipe.

BETTER BEANS.
Add 2 teaspoons of vinegar to the pot when cooking dried beans. It will make them tender and easier on the digestive system, thus producing less stomach gas.

COLORFUL BEETS.
Add a little vinegar to the water in which you cook beets to keep them from fading.

OIL FIRST, THEN VINEGAR.
When mixing oil and vinegar into a salad, put the oil in first, then add the vinegar. If you put the vinegar in first, the oil tends to slip off the lettuce.

CLEAR VINEGAR.

Add ¼ teaspoon of salt to your vinegar cruet, and the vinegar will stay clear.

KETCHUP STRETCHER.

Before discarding that ketchup bottle, rinse it out with a little vinegar. Add the vinegar-and-ketchup mixture to French or Thousand Island salad dressing.

WHITE CAULIFLOWER.

To make cauliflower white, add 1 tablespoon vinegar to the water you boil or steam the vegetable in. This is especially important if the cauliflower is not at its freshest. The vinegar will improve its appearance and taste.

SOUR CREAM SUBSTITUTE.

If you don't have sour cream on hand, you can make a sour cream substitute by adding 4 teaspoons vinegar to 1 cup heavy cream.

BETTER OKRA.

To keep okra from "roping" (becoming stringy and tough) while cooking, add a tablespoon of vinegar to the cooking water.

FRESHER COTTAGE CHEESE.

A teaspoon of vinegar added to a carton of cottage cheese will keep it fresh right down to the last spoonful, without altering the flavor.

BETTER DOUGHNUTS.

To keep homemade doughnuts from becoming soggy, add a tablespoon of vinegar to the frying fat. The vinegar keeps the doughnuts from becoming greasy.

ZESTY SOUP.

Make vegetable or bean soups taste better by adding 1 teaspoon of red wine vinegar just before serving. It gives the soups a zesty zip.

PERK UP CANNED FOOD.

Add a teaspoon of red wine vinegar to canned gravy, soup, or sauces. The vinegar adds flavor and makes the canned food taste fresher.

SAUCE FOR FISH.

Heavy cream combined with white wine vinegar makes a wonderful sauce for fish. Combine 2 teaspoons white wine vinegar to ½ cup unsweetened heavy cream. Serve drizzled over baked, grilled, poached, or smoked fish.

CANNED SHRIMP.

Soak canned shrimp in a little sherry and 2 tablespoons of vinegar for 15 minutes for a fresher taste.

FRUIT FLAVOR.

Sprinkle white vinegar on fresh cantaloupe or canned fruit to perk the fruit up and bring out the flavor.

FRUIT DRESSING.

Create a tasty pink dressing for fruit and fruit salad by stirring 2 tablespoons strawberry or raspberry vinegar into 1 cup plain yogurt or sour cream.

STRAWBERRIES WITH ZIP.

Give ripe strawberries a sweet, mouthwatering tang. In a large bowl, gently mix 1 pint sliced strawberries with 4 tablespoons sugar. Let stand for thirty minutes. Add 1 tablespoon balsamic vinegar, stir, and serve immediately.

LEMON SUBSTITUTE.

You can save money by substituting vinegar for lemon juice in any recipe unless you really need the lemon flavor. Use ½ teaspoon vinegar for each teaspoon of lemon juice called for in the recipe.

EASY-CUT GELATIN.

Add 1 tablespoon vinegar to each package of gelatin. It improves the texture and makes it easier to cut.

FIRM GELATIN.

During the summer molded gelatin salads and desserts can tend to melt in the heat. Add 1 teaspoon of vinegar per box of gelatin, and your recipes will hold up to the heat.

STRETCH SALAD DRESSING.

To save money and calories mix 1 part vinegar to 1 part oil when making oil-and-vinegar salad dressing. (The traditional combination is 1 part vinegar to 2 parts oil.) This way you'll save 20 calories and 2 grams of fat per tablespoon serving. Use a flavorful herb vinegar or balsamic vinegar.

BUTTERMILK SUBSTITUTE.

Instead of buying expensive buttermilk, put 1 tablespoon vinegar in a measuring cup. Add enough fresh milk to make one cup. Let the mixture stand until it thickens (for about 5 to 15 minutes). You can speed up the process by placing the mixture in the microwave for thirty seconds.

STORE HERBS.

Instead of drying herbs, store them in vinegar. Here's how: Loosely pack a jar with fresh herbs and add warmed vinegar to cover by 1 inch. Make sure all leaves are immersed, then cover tightly. Herbs can be stored at room temperature and used in the same proportion as dried herbs. Tarragon and basil are good choices to store in vinegar. Herbs packed in vinegar will keep for several years.

FIRM FISH FILETS.

For firmer, whiter fish, soak your fish filets for about twenty minutes in a quart of water and 2 tablespoons vinegar.

EASY-TO-SCALE FISH.

All kinds of fish are easier to scale if they are rubbed with vinegar and allowed to sit for 5 minutes beforehand.

FLAVORFUL FISH.

Add a tablespoon of vinegar to fried or boiled fish (or seafood) when cooking to bring out the flavor.

BETTER EGGS.

When boiling eggs, add 2 tablespoons of white vinegar per quart of water before boiling. This will prevent cracking, and the shells will peel off faster and more easily.

POACHED EGGS.

You don't need an expensive egg-poaching machine to make perfectly poached eggs; use an empty tuna can! Remove the top and bottom with a can opener. Drop the can in a pan of boiling water and crack an egg or two into it, and you will have beautiful poached eggs. Add a drop or two of vinegar to the boiling water before you add the eggs to keep the egg whites from spreading.

FLUFFY RICE.

To make white rice fluffy and less sticky, add 1 teaspoon of white distilled or rice vinegar to the boiling water.

MOIST CAKE.

To make any homemade or boxed chocolate cake recipe moist and fluffier, add a spoonful of vinegar to the dry ingredients. You'll be amazed at the difference.

MEAT TENDERIZER.

Meat fibers are broken down and tenderized by vinegar. Less expensive, lean cuts of meat can be used in most recipes without sacrificing flavor. Soak the meat in vinegar overnight. If desired, rinse off the vinegar before cooking.

TAME THE GAME.

Improve the flavor of wild game by soaking the meat in a mixture of half vinegar and half water for at least one hour before cooking.

NO MORE DRY OR MOLDY CHEESE.

To prevent cheese from drying out and molding, wrap it in a moist paper towel with a small amount of cider vinegar. Store the cheese in a sealed plastic bag or airtight container. You may need to add water or a drop or two of cider vinegar to keep the towel damp.

WHITE MASHED POTATOES.

Vinegar makes mashed potatoes stay white. First add the milk to the boiled potatoes and mix to the consistency you desire. Next add 1 teaspoon vinegar for each pound of potatoes, then beat the potatoes for one more minute.

AVOID UNPLEASANT ODORS.

When cooking vegetables such as cauliflower that give off an unpleasant odor, simmer a small pan of vinegar on top of the stove while the vegetables are cooking, or simply add a little vinegar to the cooking water.

SEASON POTS AND PANS.

Protect frying pans by boiling vinegar in them. This will prevent foods from sticking to the pan for several months. When you notice that foods are starting to stick to the pan, repeat the process.

FRIED FOODS.

Make fried foods taste less greasy by adding a tablespoon of vinegar to the pan or deep fryer before adding the oil.

DISH TOO SALTY?

If you add too much salt to a recipe, don't toss it out; add a teaspoon of cider vinegar and a teaspoon of sugar to eliminate the salty taste.

TOO MUCH SUGAR?

If you add too much sugar to a main dish or vegetable recipe add a teaspoon of cider vinegar to save the dish.

WINE SUBSTITUTE.

When a recipe calls for wine, you can substitute vinegar. Simply dilute 1 part vinegar to 3 parts of water.

GARLIC SUBSTITUTE.

Use garlic vinegar instead of fresh garlic in any recipe: 1 teaspoon is the equivalent of a small clove of garlic. (See Basic Recipe for Vegetable Vinegar, page 110, to make garlic vinegar, or you can buy garlic vinegar at the grocery store or health food store.)

SEAFOOD TENDERIZER.

Muscle fiber in salmon, lobster, oysters, and other fish is tenderized by the acid in vinegar. Soak the seafood in vinegar for several hours or overnight. If desired, rinse off the vinegar before cooking.

BETTER SWEETS.

Add a teaspoon of vinegar to baked pies, cakes, and other sweet desserts to enhance the flavor and make the texture lighter.

SHINY FROSTING.

Add ½ teaspoon vinegar to homemade frosting to make the texture soft and creamy. White frosting will look very white and shiny.

MARVELOUS MERINGUE.

Make perfect meringue every time by adding vinegar to the egg whites. Add ½ teaspoon vinegar to every 3 egg whites used. Your meringue will be very fluffy, yet stable.

MAYONNAISE AND SALAD-DRESSING RETRIEVAL.

Get the last remaining contents of mayonnaise or salad dressing out of the jar by adding a little vinegar and shaking the jar.

BEAUTIFUL BREAD.

Ensure that your homemade bread has the most beautiful crust by brushing the top of the bread with vinegar ten minutes before the bread is done. Just remove the bread from the oven, brush vinegar on top, and return it to the hot oven to finish baking.

HIGH-RISING BREAD.

Add 1 tablespoon of vinegar for every 2½ cups flour when adding other liquids to a bread recipe. (Be sure to reduce the liquids by the amount of vinegar added.) This will help your bread rise, giving it a delicious texture.

SAVE WILTED VEGETABLES.

To revive wilted vegetables, quickly dunk them in hot tap water, then place them in a bowl of ice water with a tablespoon of cider or white vinegar.

HEALTHY STEAMED VEGETABLES.

Add 2 tablespoons of vinegar to the water used for steaming vegetables. Your vegetables will retain more color and vitamins, and the vinegar will eliminate any unpleasant odors.

TENDER VEGETABLES.

Cellulose can be broken down with vinegar. Add a 2 tea-spoons vinegar to the water when cooking fibrous or stringy veg-etables such as beets, cabbage, celery, or spinach. Sprinkle a few drops of vinegar on raw vegetables such as lettuce, broccoli, car-rots, cucumbers, or kale immediately before serving.

NO MORE DISCOLORED PRODUCE.

Keep cut apples, pears, and avocados from browning and potatoes from turning black by dipping them into a small bowl of water with 2 tablespoons of vinegar added. Or you can simply soak the produce in the vinegar water until you are ready to use them.

CLEAN FRESH PRODUCE.

Wash vegetables and fruit in water with vinegar added to remove any dirt, insects, pesticides, or residues. Use 3 table-spoons of vinegar to a gallon of water.

BETTER BOILED HAM.

Add 2 tablespoons of white or cider vinegar to the water that you boil ham in. It will draw out some of the salty taste and accentuate the flavor.

WEIGHT-LOSS HELPER.

Sprinkling a little vinegar on cooked foods (such as meat or vegetables) will take the edge off your appetite and cause you to eat less. A simple salad with vinegar dressing will do the trick.

SPAGHETTI-SAUCE-FLAVOR BOOSTER.
Add 1 tablespoon of vinegar to homemade or store-bought spaghetti sauce to improve the flavor.

■ Pickles ■

Pickles and relishes are whole, sliced, or chopped fruits or vegetables preserved in a vinegar-sugar mixture. If the label of a packaged food says it is pickled, by law the product must be put up in vinegar. Pickling is one of the most basic and easiest ways to preserve foods. It works by increasing the acidity of foods to a level at which bacteria cannot thrive. Expect a batch of pickled vegetables to last a month or two in the refrigerator. If canned, they will last over a year.

Because pickles are already partially preserved, they do not have to be canned in a pressure cooker. A boiling-water bath provides enough heat to seal and sterilize them. Care does need to be taken in choosing utensils and pans with which to make pickles. The high acid content reacts with some metals such as aluminum and iron. It is better to use enamel, glass, or stainless steel pans and plastic or wooden utensils.

PICKLING TIPS.
Cider vinegar or any other vinegar with a mild flavor is good for pickling. Be sure that the label indicates that the vinegar has at least 4 to 6 percent acidity, or your pickled vegetables may spoil. Do not use homemade or commercial vinegar that has an unknown acidity. (See page 104.) Although cider vinegar may darken pickles slightly, it is nice for its pleasantly mild flavor. White vinegar has a sharper taste, but should be used when pickling light-colored foods such as pears, cauliflower, and onions.

Don't dilute vinegar when making pickles; if the mixture seems too sour, add sugar to achieve the proper balance.

Always use fresh, firm young vegetables or fruits, because they will make the crunchiest and most flavorful pickled food. Wash them very carefully and cut away any bad spots. Slightly under-ripe vegetables will produce crisper pickles.

Avoid bruised or molding vegetables and fruit. These will frequently result in poor-quality pickles.

Never store cucumbers that you intend to pickle in the refrigerator. They start to deteriorate if stored below 50 degrees.

For best flavor, cucumbers should be used within twenty-four hours of harvest.

For the best taste, cut off both ends of cucumbers. The blossom end (opposite end from the stem) contains concentrated enzymes that can soften pickles.

When a pickle recipe calls for cucumbers, make sure to choose cucumbers that have not been waxed. The waxed skins will not absorb the liquid.

The water used when pickling should be naturally soft or artificially softened. If you have hard water, soften it by boiling slightly more than the desired amount of water in a stainless steel or uncracked enamel pan for fifteen minutes. Remove the water from the heat, cover it, and allow it to set for twenty-four hours. Remove any film or scum that may have formed. Slowly pour the water from the container, making sure that the mineral settlement stays at the bottom of the pan. Measure the water again before adding to the recipe.

Do not use table salt for making pickles. Use only pickling salt, kosher salt, or other salt that says on the label that it is non-iodized.

Rock salt or other salts used to melt ice from roads and sidewalks must not be used for pickling.

Do not use copper, brass, iron, or galvanized utensils, which may react unfavorably with the acid in the vinegar and the salt. Plastic or wooden utensils work best.

Never boil vinegar for pickles any longer than absolutely necessary. Acetic acid evaporates at boiling temperatures, which can make the vinegar too weak to do a good job of preserving the pickled food.

Buy fresh spices at the beginning of the pickling and canning season. Spices tend to deteriorate and should be discarded at the beginning of the next pickling season.

Be accurate when measuring ingredients. Too little of one ingredient and too much of another could result in pickles that are unsafe to eat.

When reusing jars, discard those with chipped or nicked necks because they won't form a tight seal. Make sure the sealing compound on new metal lids is even and smooth. You can reuse screw bands as long they are not bent or rusty and are otherwise in good condition.

After canning, wipe off the outside of each jar with white vinegar after the jars are sealed and cooled. This will keep mold from appearing during storage.

Pickles derive their flavor from their marinating solution. Experiment with spices and make your pickles to suit your taste buds.

Traditionally, pickled foods are served at the beginning of a meal because they stimulate the flow of saliva and gastric juices. They make other foods taste better.

DIRECTIONS FOR WATER-BATH PROCESSING OF PICKLES.

To process pickled foods using the water-bath method, you will need a large kettle with a cover (lid) and a rack. Choose a deep kettle that can hold the jars plus enough water to cover them by 1 to 2 inches. You will also need a jar lifter and a ladle.

When preparing pickles with the water-bath processing, work quickly and do not prepare more food than you can process at one time in the water bath. Hot jars will break with temperature changes; do not place them on cold surfaces or leave them in a drafty area.

1. Examine tops and edges of standard jars to see that there are no cracks, nicks, or sharp edges on the sealing surfaces.
2. Wash jars in hot soapy water or run through the dishwasher.
3. Cover jars with hot water and leave them in the hot water until ready to use.

4. Pour or pack prepared ingredients into hot pint or half-pint jars, leaving a ¼-inch space at the top.

5. Wipe the rims, put on two-piece lids, and fasten the screw bands.

6. Put the jars on a rack in a deep kettle half full of boiling water and add more boiling water to cover the lids by 1 to 2 inches. Leave enough space between jars for water to circulate around them.

7. Cover the pot, bring to a hard boil, reduce the heat to hold the water at a steady but gentle boil, and continue to boil for 15 minutes. Remove the jars from the boiling water with a jar lifter.

8. Cool, remove bands, and label. Store jars in a cool, dark place.

9. Let the flavors blend for at least a month before using. Refrigerate after opening.

PROBLEM PICKLES?

Pickled foods are easy to make and can withstand several variations in the course of processing. But occasionally they may not turn out exactly as you had hoped. The finished pickled product may not be perfect. A vinegar solution that is too strong or too weak, or adding the wrong amount of sugar or salt can make the pickled food mushy and limp instead of crisp and crunchy. Contact with minerals can cause your pickled foods to have a strange color. Pickling foods is just like other types of cooking: The more often you pickle foods, the better results you will have. Use this guide to diagnose any problems you encounter while pickling foods.

GUIDE TO PICKLED FOODS.

If:	The pickles can be:
Vinegar mixture is too strong	Tough, shriveled
Too much salt is added	Tough
Too much sugar is added	Shriveled
Brine (salt solution) is too weak	Soft

If:	The pickles can be:
Table salt is used (it contains starch)	Cloudy
Old cucumbers are used	Hollow
Cooked in a copper kettle	Off Color
Water has high mineral content	Off Color
Time in brine (salt solution) is inadequate	Slippery
Cooked too long	Mushy

■ Favorite Pickle Recipes ■

BREAD-AND-BUTTER PICKLES

5 medium cucumbers
3 medium onions
½ cup salt
¼ cup vinegar
1 cup water
½ teaspoon celery seed
½ teaspoon mustard seed
¾ cup sugar
½ teaspoon ginger
¼ teaspoon turmeric

1. Wash the cucumbers and cut them into thin slices. Peel and slice the onions. Combine the cucumbers and onions in a large bowl. Add the salt and let the mixture stand for 2 hours, then drain.
2. Bring the vinegar, water, celery seed, mustard seed, sugar, ginger, and turmeric to a boil. Add the cucumbers and onions. Boil slowly until tender.
3. Follow directions on page 132 for the water-bath method of preserving.

Makes two or three half-pints.

GARLIC-DILL PICKLES

about 4 pounds thin, pickling cucumbers
6 cloves garlic
12 sprigs fresh dill
1 quart cider vinegar
1 quart water
½ cup noniodized salt
six sterilized canning jars

1. Wash the cucumbers. Cut off and discard a thin slice from each end. Place in a bowl of cold water. Cover and refrigerate for 12 hours or overnight.
2. In each of the six sterilized canning jars, place a garlic clove, 2 sprigs of dill, and enough cucumbers to fill.
3. In a large nonreactive kettle, combine vinegar, water, and salt. Bring to a boil over high heat and stir until the salt is dissolved (about 2 minutes).
4. Follow directions on page 132 for the water-bath method of preserving.

Makes 6 pints.

CHUNK PICKLES

24 cucumbers (each about 3 inches long)
½ cup pickling salt
8 cups water
2½ cups sugar
2 cups vinegar
¼ cup mustard seed
1 tablespoon celery seed
1 teaspoon curry powder

1. Wash the cucumbers, cut them into 1-inch cubes, and place them in a large bowl. Dissolve the salt in water and pour it over the cucumbers. Cover the bowl and let it stand at room temperature for 5 hours.

2. Drain the cucumbers, rinse them thoroughly, and place them in a large kettle.

3. In a large saucepan, bring the remaining ingredients to a boil, stirring until the sugar is melted. Pour the mixture over the cucumbers and bring to a boil.

4. Fill the jars, following directions on page 132 for the water-bath method of preserving.

Makes 5 or 6 half-pints.

PICKLED ONIONS

4 quarts small white pickling onions, peeled and left whole
1 cup pickling salt
2 quarts white vinegar
2 cups sugar
¼ cup mustard seed
2 tablespoons prepared horseradish
white peppercorns
bay leaves
pimento slices

1. Sprinkle the onions with the salt. Cover them with cold water and let stand for 6 hours or overnight. Rinse thoroughly with cold water and drain well.

2. Combine the vinegar, sugar, mustard seed, and horseradish in a pot and simmer for 10 minutes.

3. Spoon the onions into hot sterilized jars, adding a few peppercorns, a bay leaf, and some pimento slices to each jar.

4. Pour the boiling hot vinegar mixture over the onions, leaving a ½-inch space at the top.

5. Close the jar and follow directions on page 132 for the water-bath method of preserving.

Makes about 8 pints.

GREEN-TOMATO PICKLES

2 ½ cups white vinegar
2 cups sugar
¼ cup dill seed
1 tablespoon mustard seed
1 tablespoon celery seed
1 tablespoon pickling salt
5 pounds green tomatoes, washed and cored
1 large onion, thinly sliced

1. In a large saucepan, combine the vinegar, sugar, dill seed, mustard seed, celery seed, and pickling salt. Bring to a boil.
2. Cut the tomatoes into slices about ⅜ inch thick, discarding end pieces. Add the tomatoes and onion to the boiling syrup.
3. Reduce the heat and simmer for 10 minutes, stirring occasionally.
4. Immediately fill hot, sterilized jars with tomatoes and onion, leaving a ½-inch space at the top of each jar. Immediately pour the hot syrup over the tomatoes, leaving ½-inch space at the top of each jar.
5. Carefully run a nonmetallic utensil down the inside of the jars to remove trapped air bubbles. Wipe tops and threads of jars clean. Place hot lids on jars and screw the bands on firmly.
6. Follow directions on page 132 for the water-bath method of preserving.

Makes 5 or 6 half-pints.

PIMENTOS

4 large red peppers
1 cup white vinegar
1 cup water
⅓ cup sugar
3 garlic cloves, chopped
2 teaspoons vegetable oil
1 teaspoon salt

1. Wash the peppers, remove the seeds, and slice them into inch-wide strips.
2. Cover the peppers with boiling water and let them soak for 5 minutes. Drain.
3. Combine the vinegar, water, and sugar in a glass or enamel pan and bring to a boil. Simmer the mixture for 5 minutes, then remove from the heat and add the garlic, oil, and salt.
4. Place the peppers in a clean quart-sized jar and pour the vinegar mixture over them to cover. Store pimentos in the refrigerator for at least 2 weeks before using.

Makes 1 quart.

SPICED PICKLED EGGS

12 small eggs, hard boiled and peeled
1 small onion, thinly sliced
3 cups vinegar
1 cinnamon stick
1 tablespoon honey
1 teaspoon whole allspice
1 teaspoon whole cloves
½ teaspoon whole coriander seed
1 bay leaf
1 small slice of fresh ginger (optional)

1. Place the eggs and onion in a widemouthed jar.

2. In a glass or enamel saucepan, combine the remaining ingredients and bring the mixture to a boil. Reduce heat and simmer for 5 minutes.
3. Remove from the heat and pour the liquid over the eggs.
4. Cover the jar and refrigerate for at least 10 days before serving. Eggs will keep about 2 months in the refrigerator.

Makes 12 pickled eggs.

PENNSYLVANIA DUTCH PICKLED PIGS' FEET

4 pigs' feet
3 cups vinegar
1 onion, sliced
12 whole peppercorns
6 whole cloves
1 bay leaf
1 tablespoon salt

1. Split the pigs' feet apart with your fingers so that you can scrub them thoroughly, then place them in a large saucepan and cover with cold water. Add the vinegar and bring to a boil. Skim the foam off the top before adding additional ingredients.

2. Add the onion and seasonings and heat to boiling, then reduce heat to a low simmer for 2 hours.

3. Let the mixture cool in its cooking liquid. Do not drain the liquid.

4. Refrigerate and serve chilled.

5. Pickled pigs' feet will keep several weeks in the refrigerator.

Makes a "mess" of pickled pigs' feet (about 4 cups).

SUMMERTIME SQUASH PICKLES

⅔ cup pickling salt
2 quarts water
4 cups thinly sliced yellow squash
1¼ cups sugar
1 cup vinegar
1 teaspoon mustard seed
1 medium onion, thinly sliced
1 green pepper, halved, seeded, and thinly sliced

1. In a large bowl, stir the salt into the water. Add the squash and weigh them down with a dinner plate and an unopened can to keep the squash submerged in the brine. Let stand 3 hours; drain well.
2. Combine the sugar, vinegar, and mustard seed in a large pot. Bring to boil and continue to boil until the sugar is melted. Add the drained squash, onion, and pepper. Return just to boiling, remove from heat, and cool.
3. Transfer to a large container with a tight-fitting lid. Refrigerate. These will keep several weeks.

Makes 2½ quarts.

SPICED PEARS

4 to 5 pounds firm pears, peeled, halved, and cored
vinegar water (2 quarts water plus 2 tablespoons white vinegar)
4 cinnamon sticks, broken into small pieces
1 whole nutmeg, chopped
3 cups sugar
1½ cups white vinegar
1 cup water

1. Place the pears in a bowl filled with the vinegar water to prevent browning.

2. Tie the cinnamon and nutmeg in a spice bag or cheesecloth.
3. In a large saucepan, combine the sugar, vinegar, water, and spice bag. Bring to a boil. Reduce heat and simmer for 5 minutes.
4. Drain the pears and add them to the syrup. Simmer for 5 to 10 minutes, or until pears are tender but still firm. Remove the spice bag.
5. Immediately fill hot jars with pears, leaving ½-inch head space. Pour the hot syrup over pears, leaving ½-inch head space. Carefully run a nonmetallic utensil down the inside of the jars to remove trapped air bubbles. Wipe tops and threads of jars clean. Place hot lids on jars and screw the bands on firmly.
6. Follow directions on page 132 for the water-bath method of preserving.

Makes 4 or 5 pints.

PICKLED CRANBERRIES WITH ORANGE AND MINT

3 cups white vinegar
3½ cups sugar
1½ cups water
2 tablespoons fresh orange zest, finely grated
7 cups fresh cranberries
½ cup fresh mint, minced

1. In a large nonreactive pan, combine the vinegar, sugar, water, and orange zest. Bring mixture to a boil over medium heat, stirring frequently. Reduce heat to a simmer and continue to cook for 5 minutes, stirring often.
2. Add the cranberries and cook for five to 7 minutes, or until skins have popped open. Stir in the mint.
3. Follow directions on page 132 for the water-bath method of preserving.

Makes 3 pints.

WATERMELON RIND PICKLES

These may not sound like they will taste good, but after you try them, you'll never throw away the rinds again!

> 2 pounds watermelon rind (about 2 quarts or one large
>   watermelon)
> 3 tablespoons pickling salt
> 2 quarts cold water, divided
> 1 tablespoon alum
> 4½ cups sugar
> 2 cups white vinegar
> ⅓ cup whole cloves
> 1 cinnamon stick

1. To prepare the watermelon rind, peel and remove all green and pink flesh. Cut into 1-inch cubes and place in a large bowl.
2. Dissolve the salt in 1 quart of the water and pour it over rind cubes. Let stand for 24 hours, then drain thoroughly.
3. In a large pot, dissolve the alum in the remaining quart of water and pour it over the rind. Let stand for 24 hours, then drain thoroughly and cover with fresh water. Let stand for 24 hours.
4. Bring the rind to a boil in this water. Boil gently for 45 minutes or until tender. Drain.
5. In a separate pot, combine the sugar and vinegar. Tie the spices in a cheesecloth bag, and add them to the sugar-and-vinegar mixture. Simmer about 10 minutes. Add the watermelon rind. Cook for 30 to 40 minutes until the rind chunks are clear and tender. Remove and discard the spice bag.
6. Pack boiling hot into sterilized jars. Follow directions on page 132 for the water-bath method of preserving.

Makes 3 or 4 pints.

In the following recipes you may use apple cider vinegar, unless the recipe calls for a different type of vinegar. For a unique flavor, substitute any of your favorite herb or flavored vinegars.

■ Condiments and Sauces ■

OLD-FASHIONED SPICY MUSTARD

This recipe is from the 1870s. Its wonderful taste is similar to that of store-bought gourmet mustard.

> 1 quart cider vinegar
> 2 tablespoons ground allspice
> 2 tablespoons cinnamon
> 1 tablespoon cloves
> 3 tablespoons brown sugar
> 4 tablespoons salt
> 3 onions, minced or cut fine
> 1 pound of ground mustard seed (see note)

1. Combine all ingredients except mustard seed in a saucepan and simmer over low heat until the flavors are extracted, about half an hour. Strain the vinegar, discarding the flavorings.
2. Add the flavored vinegar a little at a time to the mustard seed until you get the desired consistency.
3. Store the mustard in a glass jar in the refrigerator. It keeps wells, and the flavor improves with age.

NOTE: Mustard seed can be powdered with a mortar and pestle.

HOMEMADE KETCHUP (CATSUP)

1 can (8 ounces) tomato sauce
¼ cup sugar
dash of cinnamon
1 tablespoon vinegar

Pour the tomato sauce into a small saucepan and boil away some of the water until it begins to thicken. Then add the sugar, cinnamon, and vinegar. Simmer for 3 to 4 minutes more. Refrigerate.

Makes 8 ounces.

NEW YORK ONION-TOMATO HOT DOG TOPPING

2 large onions, cut into quarters and thinly sliced (about 2
  cups)
⅓ cup ketchup (homemade or store bought)
1 tablespoon water
1 tablespoon cider vinegar
¾ teaspoon sugar

Simmer all ingredients together until the onions are translucent. Store in a covered container in the refrigerator.

Makes ½ cup.

TABASCO-TYPE HOT SAUCE

hot red peppers
garlic, if desired
white vinegar

Remove the stem ends from as many hot red peppers as you want to use. Chop the peppers coarsely. Cook the peppers in just enough water to keep them from sticking to the pot, until they turn soft (about 10 minutes). Add chopped garlic, if desired. Put the soft peppers and garlic into a blender or through a food mill or sieve. Measure the puree. Measure out the same amount of white vinegar. Pour the vinegar into a nonreactive saucepan and bring to a boil, then add the hot pepper puree. Stir to combine and remove from heat. Cool, seal in bottles, and refrigerate.

SUN-DRIED TOMATOES

Dried tomatoes add a rich flavor to pastas, sautéed vegetables, salads, and sauces. They are very expensive to buy but easy to make at home. Grow your own tomatoes or dry them when tomatoes are in season and priced low. Most regions of the United States do not have the hot, dry air necessary to sun-dry tomatoes. If you have a food dehydrator, you can use it to dry tomatoes, but if not, your oven will work just fine.

> plum tomatoes
> salt
> vinegar
> olive oil
> garlic, if desired

Cut the tomatoes in half and remove the stem ends. Lay them cut side up on nonreactive (nonaluminum) baking sheets. Lightly salt. Place in an oven turned on to the lowest possible temperature. Drying time will depend on the oven, humidity, and juiciness of the tomatoes. They are dried when they are shriveled and have a leathery, prunelike texture. Dip each tomato half in vinegar, shaking off the excess, and then place in a sterilized canning jar. Pack each jar with tomatoes, leaving a ½-inch space at the top. Add garlic or herbs such as basil, thyme, or rosemary, if desired. Completely cover the tomatoes with olive oil. Store jars in the refrigerator.

HERB JELLY

3 cups apple juice
1 cup Herb Infusion (see recipe below)
2 tablespoons vinegar
1 package powdered pectin
4 cups white sugar
5 half-pint sterilized hot jars and lids

First make the herb infusion, which is actually a strong tea.

HERB INFUSION

Take one cup of washed, towel-dried, and well-packed herbs of your choice. Mint, basil, sage, parsley, lavender, and tarragon are some of my favorites. Place herbs into a stainless or glass pan with a lid. Pour one cup of boiling water over the herbs and let steep, covered for about one hour. Keep the water hot but do not boil. Strain out the leaves, using a double layer of cheesecloth. Cool to room temperature.

Continue with the jelly recipe.

In a large pan, mix all the ingredients together except the sugar. Stir constantly until the mixture comes to a full boil. Add the sugar all at once and keep stirring until the mixture comes to a full boil; continue to boil one minute. Remove the jelly from the heat.

Pour into hot jars, seal, and process in a simmering water bath for 15 minutes. To make the jelly easy to recognize, place one clean herb leaf in each jar. For more directions and information on canning and sealing jars, see Pickles on page 130.

Makes 5 half-pints.

GARLIC JELLY

If you love garlic, you'll love this recipe. The garlic flavor really stands out.

> *½ cup finely chopped garlic (about 15 to 20 large cloves)*
> *3 cups white wine vinegar*
> *2 cups water*
> *2 boxes (2 ounce each) powdered pectin*
> *food coloring (optional)*

1. In a 2-quart or larger pan, combine the garlic and vinegar. Simmer gently, uncovered, over medium heat for 15 minutes. Remove from the heat and pour into a quart jar. Cover and let stand at room temperature for 24 to 36 hours.
2. Pour the flavored vinegar through a strainer into a bowl, pressing the garlic with the back of a spoon to squeeze out the liquid. Measure the liquid and add more vinegar if necessary to make 2 cups. Discard the garlic.
3. In a 5- to 6-quart kettle, combine the flavored vinegar and pectin. Bring to a full boil over medium-high heat, then stir in the sugar. Boil for 2 minutes, stirring constantly.
4. If desired, stir in 2 drops of red, orange, or yellow food coloring. Skim off the foam, then spoon the hot jelly into half-pint jars to within 1 inch of rim. Seal. Process in a simmering water bath 15 minutes. For more directions and information on canning and sealing jars, see Pickles on page 130.

Makes 5 or 6 half-pints.

BARBECUE SAUCE

2 cups ketchup
4 tablespoons Worcestershire sauce
2 teaspoons chili powder
1 cup water
4 tablespoons cider vinegar
2 tablespoons brown sugar
1 teaspoon salt
½ teaspoon pepper
2 tablespoons minced onion

Combine all the ingredients in a saucepan. Cook over medium heat for 20 minutes. Reduce the heat to low, cover, and cook for 30 minutes. Remove from the heat. Allow the mixture to cool. Pour into a large jar and refrigerate.

Microwave oven directions: Combine all ingredients in a glass bowl and cover with plastic wrap. Cook on high for 10 minutes. Lower the setting to medium and cook an additional 10 minutes.

Crock-pot Directions: Combine all ingredients in Crock-pot and stir well. Cover and cook on low for 4 to 5 hours.

Makes about 3½ cups.

RAISIN SAUCE FOR HAM

½ cup brown sugar
1 tablespoon flour
1 tablespoon honey
1½ cups water
½ cup apple cider vinegar
½ cup raisins

Mix all ingredients together in a saucepan and simmer for 10 minutes. Brush this sauce over a ham or ham slice before cooking. Thicken the sauce and pan drippings to make a delicious gravy to serve with the ham.

Makes about 3 cups.

MEAT MARINADE

Use this marinade to tenderize and flavor meat.

> ½ cup vinegar
> 2 cups broth
> 1 medium onion, very finely chopped or grated
> 2 cloves garlic, crushed
> 1 tablespoon Worcestershire sauce
> 1 tablespoon mustard (dry or prepared)
> 2 whole cloves
> 1 bay leaf
> 1 tablespoon oregano
> 1 tablespoon soy sauce

Combine all ingredients. Pour the mixture over meat; refrigerate for 24 hours or longer. Turn the meat several times during the process. When ready to cook the meat, strain the marinade if necessary and use some or all of it as part of the liquid used in cooking the meat. Use this marinade for stews, pot roasts, and other meat dishes.

Makes about 2½ cups marinade.

APRICOT-BALSAMIC DIPPING SAUCE FOR CHICKEN

Use to dip chicken wings or to baste chicken during the last few minutes of cooking.

> 1 cup apricot preserves
> 2 tablespoons balsamic vinegar
> 1 tablespoon soy sauce

Mix together in a glass bowl.

Makes about 1 cup.

CHINESE DUCK SAUCE

2 tablespoons applesauce
½ cup orange marmalade or apricot jam
5 tablespoons cider vinegar
1 teaspoon sugar

In a bowl, stir the applesauce into the orange marmalade or apricot jam and then add the vinegar and sugar. Use a wire whisk to mix the ingredients together. Sauce will keep for 6 months in the refrigerator.

Use as a sauce on Chinese foods such as egg rolls, Chinese noodles, batter-fried vegetables, or sweet-and-sour meat pieces.

Makes about 1 cup.

CHINESE MUSTARD SAUCE

4 tablespoons dry mustard
½ teaspoon corn oil
4 teaspoons vinegar

Combine all ingredients and stir thoroughly. If the sauce is too thick, add a few drops of vinegar until you get the perfect consistency.

Makes about ½ cup.

FRESH TOMATO SAUCE

2 cups fresh tomatoes, peeled, seeded, and chopped
¼ cup vinegar
½ cup fresh parsley, minced
2 tablespoons fresh basil, minced
2 cloves garlic, minced
1 teaspoon salt
½ teaspoon black pepper
½ cup olive oil

In a large glass bowl, combine all ingredients except the oil. Add the oil in a thin stream, whisking continually until it is well mixed.

This sauce can be served hot or cold; but for the best flavor, serve at room temperature. Serve over pasta and grilled fish or chicken.

Makes about 2½ cups.

BÉARNAISE SAUCE

2 egg yolks, well beaten
1½ teaspoons lemon juice
4 tablespoons butter
2 tablespoons cream
1 teaspoon crushed tarragon
1 teaspoon chopped parsley
1 tablespoon vinegar
1 teaspoon minced onion
¼ teaspoon salt
dash dry mustard

In top of a double boiler, over boiling water, place egg yolks, lemon juice, and half the butter. Cook, stirring constantly, until the mixture begins to thicken. Remove from heat and add the remaining butter, cream, and seasonings, stirring well. Return to the top of the double boiler and continue cooking until thickened. Serve at once.

Microwave Oven Directions: Place butter in a glass bowl and cook in a microwave oven until melted (about 30 seconds on high setting). Add remaining ingredients and mix well. Return to the microwave oven and cook on medium setting for 1 to 1½ minutes or until thickened, stirring twice. Beat with a wire whisk or beater until fluffy. Serve with eggs, fish, or vegetables.

Makes about ½ cup.

QUICK AND EASY BEAN RELISH

This makes a very tasty and colorful relish.

> *1 onion, chopped*
> *1 cup vinegar*
> *1 can red kidney beans*

In a bowl, add the onion and vinegar to the kidney beans and let stand for at least one hour. Drain off the liquid and serve cold.

APPLE CHUTNEY

> *1 teaspoon salt*
> *½ pound raisins*
> *½ pound onions, finely chopped*
> *6 cups (about 12 large) apples, chopped*
> *1 cup brown sugar*
> *2 cups water*
> *1 cup apple cider vinegar*
> *1 teaspoon cinnamon*
> *½ teaspoon ginger*
> *½ teaspoon nutmeg*

Mix all the ingredients together, adding more spices if needed. Cook over medium heat until apples are soft. Pour into sterilized jars. If you are not familiar with canning, see Pickles on page 130 for more information.

APPLE BUTTER

This makes a spicy apple butter that's hard to beat. Spread apple butter on toast or biscuits for a special treat. Decorated jars of apple butter also make nice, inexpensive gifts.

> *6 pounds (about 12 large) cooking apples*

5 cups apple cider or apple juice
1 cup cider vinegar
2 cups sugar
2 cups brown sugar
3 teaspoons cinnamon
½ teaspoon nutmeg
½ teaspoon ground cloves

Combine the apples, cider (or juice), and vinegar in a large pan. Cover and simmer 30 minutes, stirring occasionally. Press through a sieve, discarding the solids. Return the apple mixture to the pan and stir in the sugars and spices. Bring the mixture to a boil, reduce the heat to low, then simmer uncovered for 2 hours or until very thick. Stir often. Keep refrigerated.

BERRY SYRUP

This syrup is perfect for pancakes, waffles, or French toast. Try it on ice cream or add a few tablespoons to a glass of water for a refreshing drink.

3 cups blueberries, strawberries, or blackberries
3 cups sugar
1 cup water
¼ cup apple cider or fruit-flavored vinegar

1. Wash and drain the berries. If using strawberries, remove the green tops. Crush the berries in a bowl. Place the puree in a glass or enamel pan and stir in the sugar and water.
2. Transfer the mixture to a saucepan and cook over medium heat for 30 minutes, stirring often. Remove from the heat and add the vinegar.
3. Strain the mixture through a coffee filter or double layer of cheesecloth and pour the syrup into a sterilized jar. Cool the syrup before using and store in the refrigerator for up to 6 months.

Makes abut 3½ to 4 cups.

GOAT'S MILK VINEGAR CHEESE

This makes a soft cheese with a texture of a ricotta or cottage cheese and the flavor is wonderful. Eat it plain or add your favorite flavorings like cinnamon, vanilla, or crushed fruit for a dessert cheese. Herbs such as chives or oregano also give it a nice flavor.

> 1 gallon goat's milk
> ⅓ cup apple cider vinegar
> 2 heaping tablespoons baking soda

Heat the goat's milk in a nonreactive pan until foaming but not boiling (about 5 minutes), then add the vinegar. Stir well. Put the pan in the sink and add baking soda. The mixture will foam up. Stir well. Place the mixture in cheesecloth and hang for about 45 minutes or until it stops dripping. Store in the refrigerator.

■ **Soups** ■

BEEF SOUP WITH A TWIST

> 2 tablespoons oil
> 2 pounds browned beef and bones
> 2½ quarts hot water
> 1 tablespoon salt
> 2 16-ounce cans shredded beets, juice reserved
> 1 onion, diced
> 3 teaspoons sugar
> ½ teaspoon pepper
> 3 tablespoons vinegar
> 2 cloves garlic, crushed

Pour the oil into a large Dutch oven and brown the meat and bones in it, slowly searing on all sides. Add the hot water and salt.

Simmer for 2 hours. Add the shredded beets with their juice and the diced onion. Cook 30 minutes longer. Add the sugar, pepper, vinegar, and crushed garlic.

Serves 6 to 8.

TURKEY SOUP

This recipe is ideal for the day after Thanksgiving.

> *1 turkey carcass*
> *2 tablespoons vinegar*
> *2 cups barley*
> *4 carrots, sliced*
> *3 stalks celery, diced*
> *2 large onions, diced*
> *1 can (28 to 32 ounces) tomatoes*

1. Cover the turkey carcass with water in a large pot, add vinegar, cover, and simmer over low heat for 2 hours. Add water if needed. The vinegar will tenderize the turkey meat, making it easy to remove from the bones as well as to draw calcium from the bones into the soup.
2. Remove the carcass and allow it to cool. Pull the turkey meat from the bones and add back to the pot with all the other ingredients except the tomatoes. Cook the soup for 1 hour. Add the tomatoes during the last 10 minutes.

Serves 6 to 8.

CHICKEN SOUP

Mom always said chicken soup would make you feel better. This recipe is fortified with vinegar, and it will get you back on your feet in no time. This soup is healthy, low in calories, and high in calcium. The vinegar leaches calcium from the chicken bones and makes a stock rich in calcium. This soup will perk you up even if you aren't "under the weather." It tastes great!

> *½ cup vinegar*
> *2 pounds chicken (boney pieces such as wings are fine)*
> *¾ cup tiny pasta*
> *2 chicken bouillon cubes*
> *2 egg whites, slightly beaten*
> *fresh parsley, optional*

1. Pour a gallon of water into a large pot. Add the vinegar and the chicken parts. Gently simmer the chicken for 2 hours, uncovered.
2. Take the chicken pieces out and let them cool down. Strain the broth and skim off the fat. Remove the chicken meat from the bones. Add the chicken meat, pasta, and bouillon cubes to the stock. Bring the soup to a boil and cook for 10 minutes.
3. Remove from the heat and quickly dribble the egg whites over the hot liquid, stirring constantly. If desired, garnish with parsley and serve hot.

Serves 6 to 8.

CREAMED GREEN BEAN AND POTATO SOUP

> *1 pound green beans*
> *2 teaspoons salt*
> *1 large potato, peeled and cubed*
> *2 tablespoons flour*

8 ounces sour cream
¼ cup vinegar

1. Wash the beans and remove the ends and strings. Cut the beans into bite-size pieces. Place them in a large pot and cover with water. Add salt. Cook, covered, for 15 minutes. Add the potato and cook for an additional 15 minutes, adding more water if needed. Let cool.
2. Mix the flour with the sour cream in a bowl and add to cooked beans and potato mixture. Stir until well blended. Stir in the vinegar.
3. Return the soup to the heat and simmer over low until hot. Do not bring to a boil.

Serves 6 to 8.

■ Salads and Dressings ■

DEPRESSION SALAD

15½-ounce can yellow hominy, drained
15½-ounce can black-eyed peas, drained
1 green pepper, chopped
1 tomato, chopped
1 small onion, chopped
2 ribs celery, chopped
¼ cup vegetable oil
¼ cup vinegar
salt and pepper to taste

Mix the ingredients well in a large bowl and serve at room temperature or cold. For a low-fat recipe, omit the vegetable oil.

Serves 12.

DANDY DANDELION SALAD AND DRESSING

In the spring, pick as many fresh new dandelion greens as you will need to make a small bowl for each person eating. Wash the greens and shake or pat dry just as you would lettuce to remove any dirt or small pests. Do not eat dandelion greens that have been treated with lawn or other chemicals. Cut the greens into bite-size pieces with a knife or with kitchen scissors.

> *1 cup canola oil*
> *⅓ cup cider vinegar*
> *1 teaspoon salt*
> *½ teaspoon pepper*

Pour the oil into a container with all the other ingredients. Cover with a lid and shake vigorously until well blended. Pour over the dandelion greens and enjoy an inexpensive treat straight from your lawn.

SWEET POTATO SALAD

> *1 pound (about 3 large) sweet potatoes*
> *2 tablespoons mustard*
> *2 tablespoons white vinegar*
> *¼ tablespoon canola oil*
> *¼ cup diced onion*
> *½ stalk celery, thinly sliced*
> *½ small red pepper, diced*
> *salt and pepper*

1. Peel sweet potatoes, rinse, and cut them into bite-size cubes. Place the cubes in a medium pan and cover with cold water. Cover the pan and bring water to a boil. Boil for 20 minutes or until the sweet potatoes are cooked.
2. In a small bowl, mix together the mustard, vinegar, and oil. Add the onion.

3. Drain the cooked sweet potatoes and place them in a serving bowl. Toss them with dressing, celery, and red pepper. Add salt and pepper to taste.

Serves 8 to 12.

MARINATED MUSHROOMS

1 pound mushrooms, cleaned and sliced ¼ inch thick
1 sweet onion, thinly sliced
2 cloves garlic, minced
1 teaspoon dry mustard
1 teaspoon salt
1 tablespoon sugar
¼ cup water
½ cup flavored vinegar*
⅓ cup olive oil
1 tablespoon fresh parsley, finely chopped

1. Put the sliced mushrooms into a large glass bowl.
2. In a separate bowl, mix the remaining ingredients.
3. Pour the dressing over the mushrooms. Refrigerate the mixture overnight and drain before serving. Serve as an appetizer or side dish.

*See Flavored-Vinegar Recipes on page 105. Raspberry, strawberry, and onion vinegars are my favorite for this recipe.

HONEY-LIME (FAT-FREE) VINAIGRETTE

This is another fat-free salad dressing with lots of taste.

> ¼ cup fresh lime juice
> 4 teaspoons honey
> 1 tablespoon rice vinegar
> ⅛ teaspoon salt

In a small bowl, with a wire whisk or fork, mix all ingredients.

Makes about ½ cup.

TOMATO-ORANGE (FAT-FREE) VINAIGRETTE

This is a fat-free salad dressing with lots of taste.

> ½ cup tomato juice
> 1 tablespoon balsamic vinegar
> ½ teaspoon grated orange peel
> ¼ teaspoon sugar
> ⅛ teaspoon black pepper, coarsely ground

In a small bowl, with a wire whisk or fork, mix all ingredients.

Makes about ½ cup.

BALSAMIC VINAIGRETTE

> 2 cloves garlic, peeled and minced
> ½ cup balsamic vinegar
> 1 teaspoon black pepper, freshly ground
> ¾ cup olive oil
> 10 basil leaves, washed, dried, and slivered

In a bowl, mix together the garlic, vinegar, and black pepper.

Whisk in the oil in a slow, steady stream until the vinaigrette is thickened. Stir in the basil.

Makes about 1½ cups.

WATERMELON VINAIGRETTE

This is a sweet-and-sour dressing that tastes great on fruit or green salads.

> 2 tablespoons currant jelly
> ¼ cup seeded, pureed watermelon
> 2 tablespoons white wine vinegar
> ¼ teaspoon garlic pepper
> 1 teaspoon vegetable oil

1. In a small saucepan, heat the jelly until melted; cool.
2. Transfer the jelly to a bowl, add remaining ingredients, and stir until blended. Store in the refrigerator; shake well before using.

Makes about ½ cup.

HEALTHY SALAD DRESSING

This recipe is an old folk remedy that is said to promote good health. For a change of flavor, add a handful of any fresh herbs, such as basil or thyme, that you like.

> ½ cup vinegar
> ½ cup oil
> ⅓ cup honey

Mix the ingredients well and serve over lettuce with the evening meal.

Makes about 1⅓ cups.

EASY HOMEMADE MAYONNAISE

Once you taste homemade mayonnaise, you won't be without it. It tastes so much fresher than store-bought mayonnaise. It's worth the effort to make. A ham sandwich with homemade dilled mayonnaise is scrumptious!

1 fresh egg
½ teaspoon garlic salt or regular salt
1 tablespoon vinegar
1 teaspoon dry mustard
1 cup oil
dill or other fresh herb to taste, optional

In a blender, blend together the egg, salt, vinegar, and mustard with ¼ cup of the oil, for a few seconds. Then slowly add the rest of the oil while the blender is running. Store in the refrigerator for up to 3 weeks.

Makes about 1 cup.

NOTE: If you do not have a blender, a hand mixer will do the job also. Use the medium speed on the hand mixer and, if possible, get someone to help you pour in the oil as you keep the mixer going.

FRENCH SALAD DRESSING

¾ cup canola oil
¼ cup cider vinegar
¾ teaspoon coarse salt
⅛ teaspoon pepper
¼ teaspoon paprika
1 teaspoon sugar
¼ teaspoon dry mustard

Put all the ingredients in a jar and shake well.

Makes about 1 cup.

HOT MAMA SALAD DRESSING

This salad dressing is a nice change from the usual, and you can't buy anything like it in the store.

> *1 can (10¾ ounces) tomato soup*
> *1 cup cider vinegar*
> *1 cup vegetable oil*
> *salt and pepper*
> *Tabasco sauce*

Blend together the tomato soup, vinegar, and oil in a blender or beat with a hand mixer. Add salt and pepper to taste and as much Tabasco sauce as your taste buds will allow.

Makes about 3 cups.

COTTAGE CHEESE SALAD DRESSING

This is a great-tasting low-calorie salad dressing with a different taste.

> *½ cup cottage cheese*
> *3 tablespoons celery, chopped*
> *2 tablespoons onion, chopped*
> *dash of pepper*
> *1 teaspoon vinegar*
> *½ teaspoon garlic salt*

Mix all ingredients in a blender until smooth. For best flavor, chill for at least an hour before using.

Makes about ½ cup.

■ Main Dishes ■

BARBECUED FRIED CHICKEN

1 chicken, cut up for frying
salt and pepper
flour
¼ cup butter or margarine
¼ cup chopped onion
1 clove garlic
½ cup ketchup
2 drops Tabasco sauce
¼ cup water
2 tablespoons vinegar
2 tablespoons Worcestershire sauce
2 tablespoons sugar
½ teaspoon salt

Sprinkle the chicken with salt and pepper and roll it in flour. Melt the butter in a large skillet and sauté the chicken, turning to brown both sides. Remove the chicken from the skillet. Brown the onion and garlic in the fat left in skillet. Add the remaining ingredients. Place the pieces of chicken on top of the sauce, cover the skillet, and simmer for 45 minutes, or until tender. Remove the garlic clove.

Serves 4 to 6.

SPICY MEXICAN CHICKEN

This chicken is rich with the flavors of pungent cumin and allspice, of tangy vinegar, and of the earthy flavor of oregano.

½ cup cider vinegar diluted with ⅓ cup water
2 teaspoons minced garlic
1 teaspoon dried oregano, crumbled
½ teaspoon each ground allspice and ground cumin

2 medium-size red onions, thinly sliced and separated
  into rings
⅓ cup all-purpose flour
1 teaspoon salt
½ teaspoon ground red pepper (cayenne)
1 broiler or fryer chicken (about 3 pounds), quartered
¼ cup olive oil
1 can (4 ounces) chopped green chilies
½ cup cilantro leaves, chopped

1. Put the vinegar mixture, garlic, oregano, allspice, and cumin in a large bowl. Stir until well blended. Add the onion rings and toss until moistened. Let marinate while preparing the chicken.
2. Mix the flour, salt, and red pepper in a 1-gallon resealable food-storage bag. Add leg quarters to the bag and shake until well coated.
3. Heat the oil in a large deep skillet over medium-low heat. Add the leg quarters. Cook 7 to 9 minutes until well browned on one side. Meanwhile coat the breast sections in the flour mixture.
4. Turn the legs over and add the breasts to the skillet, skin side down. Continue to cook 8 minutes until browned. Turn breasts and legs over.
5. Pour the vinegar mixture from the onions into the skillet (reserve the onions). Spoon the green chilies around the chicken pieces. Bring the mixture to a boil. Reduce the heat to low; cover and simmer 15 to 20 minutes until the chicken is tender.
6. Remove the chicken to a platter and cover loosely with foil.
7. Add the onions to the sauce. Increase the heat to medium high and cook uncovered 3 to 5 minutes, stirring several times, until onions are crisp-tender.
8. Remove from the heat. Stir the cilantro into the sauce. Pour the onions and sauce over the chicken.

Serves 4.

CHICKEN BAKED IN "WINE"

The vinegar, water, and sugar give this dish its wine taste.

> *2½-3-pound broiler or fryer chicken*
> *seasoned salt*
> *2 tablespoons vinegar*
> *2 tablespoons water*
> *1 teaspoon sugar*
> *1 cup chicken broth*
> *1 tablespoon minced onion*
> *½ teaspoon curry powder*
> *2 tablespoons cornstarch*
> *4-ounce can mushrooms, drained (optional)*

1. Preheat the oven to 350 degrees.
2. Cut the chicken into serving pieces. Sprinkle lightly on both sides of each piece with seasoned salt. Place the chicken pieces skin side down in a baking dish.
3. In a bowl, mix together the vinegar, water, sugar, broth, onion, and curry powder. Pour this mixture over the chicken pieces. Cover the dish and bake for 30 minutes. Uncover the dish and turn the chicken pieces. Continue to bake 30 minutes more. Remove the chicken from the pan and skim off the fat from the meat juices.
4. In a small bowl, mix the 2 tablespoons cornstarch with ¼ cup water. Stir this mixture into the meat juices. Add mushrooms, if desired. Cook over low heat, stirring constantly, until the sauce is thickened. Spoon over the chicken before serving.

Serves 4 to 6.

VINEGAR-AND-PEPPER CHICKEN DRUMETTES

2 tablespoons balsamic vinegar
1 tablespoon plus ¼ teaspoon hot pepper sauce, divided
1 teaspoon oil
1 tablespoon honey
1½ pounds chicken wings cut into drumettes (about 30 pieces)
¼ teaspoon salt
¼ teaspoon black pepper

1. In a bowl, combine 1 tablespoon balsamic vinegar and 1 tablespoon hot pepper sauce with the oil. Put the drumettes into a resealable plastic bag, add the sauce mixture, and seal the bag. Mix the chicken in the bag to distribute the ingredients. Refrigerate overnight to marinate.
2. In a small bowl, combine the remaining tablespoon vinegar, ¼ teaspoon pepper sauce, and honey.
3. Preheat the oven to 375 degrees.
4. Place the chicken in a baking pan, sprinkle the chicken pieces with salt and pepper, and bake for 30 minutes or until the chicken next to the bone is no longer pink. Baste with the vinegar-pepper sauce mixture twice while the chicken is baking.

Serves 4 to 6.

APPLE BEEF STEW

3 tablespoons flour
1 teaspoon salt
¼ teaspoon pepper
¼ teaspoon thyme
1 pound cubed beef or veal
2 tablespoons vegetable oil
1 cup apple cider or apple juice
1 cup water
1 tablespoon vinegar
2 carrots, diced
2 potatoes, diced
1 onion, sliced
1 celery stalk, sliced
1 apple, peeled and diced

1. In a large bowl, combine flour, salt, pepper, and thyme.
2. Dredge beef or veal cubes with flour.
3. In an enameled cast-iron casserole, heat the oil to smoking and sear the beef or veal cubes. Pour off the fat.
4. Pour the apple cider or juice, water, and vinegar over beef or veal cubes. Bring the mixture to a boil, stirring constantly, then reduce the heat to medium. Cover and cook for 30 minutes or until the meat is tender.
5. Add the vegetables and apple to the simmering stew; cook 15 minutes longer or until vegetables are tender.

Serves 4 to 6.

SECOND-TIME-AROUND SANDWICHES

¼ cup chopped onion
½ cup water
½ teaspoon salt
¼ cup sugar

¼ teaspoon pepper
3 tablespoons vinegar
1 teaspoon Worcestershire sauce
½ cup ketchup
¾ cup water
leftover roast meat, sliced

Simmer the onion in ½ cup water with ½ teaspoon salt for 3 minutes. Add the sugar, pepper, vinegar, Worcestershire sauce, ketchup, and ¾ cup water. Add the meat and heat through. Serve on buns. The second time around may be a bigger hit than the original meal. Number of servings depend on the amount of leftover sliced meat.

BARBECUED SPARERIBS

2 onions, thinly sliced
4 pounds pork spareribs
2 tablespoons vinegar
2 tablespoons Worcestershire sauce
1 tablespoon salt
¼ teaspoon red pepper
½ teaspoon black pepper
1 teaspoon paprika
1 teaspoon chili powder
¾ cup ketchup
1 cup water

Preheat the oven to 350 degrees. In a 9″ x 13″ pan, arrange the sliced onions on the meat. In a small bowl, combine the remaining ingredients to make a sauce. Pour the sauce over the top of the meat. Bake 1½ hours. Baste every 15 minutes.

Serves 4 to 6.

COMPANY BEEF WITH MUSHROOMS

This recipe is easy to prepare but tastes good enough to serve for company or a special occasion. Add a fresh vegetable, some pasta, and fresh bread to complete the menu.

> 2 pounds cubed stew beef, trimmed of fat
> 2 sweet onions, sliced
> 2 tablespoons brown sugar
> 2 cups sliced mushrooms
> 1 cup beef stock
> ¼ cup apple cider vinegar or substitute garlic or fruit
>   vinegar
> 1 cup sour cream
> chopped parsley to garnish (of desired)

Preheat the oven to 300 degrees. Combine all ingredients except sour cream and parsley in a casserole dish or Dutch oven. Cover and bake for 1½ hours or until beef is fork tender. Remove the dish from the oven and stir in the sour cream. Garnish with parsley, if desired, and serve immediately.

Serves 6.

▪ Vegetables ▪

COOKED CABBAGE

> 1 head (2 to 3 pounds) cabbage
> 4 cups water
> 1 tablespoon salt
> 2 slices bacon, diced
> ½ cup flour
> ¼ cup vinegar

1. Slice the cabbage and put it in a large pot with the water and salt. Cover the pot and boil the cabbage about 1 hour until tender.

2. In a small skillet, fry the diced bacon until crisp. Remove the bacon and add the flour to the bacon grease. Fry until brown.

3. Add the flour mixture and bacon to the pot of cabbage. Mix well, then add vinegar and cook 10 to 15 minutes more. Add more salt if desired.

Serves 6 to 12.

GERMAN-STYLE GREEN BEANS

2 to 3 slices bacon, cut into ½-inch pieces
3 tablespoons onion, chopped
2 cups cooked green beans (fresh, frozen, or canned)
2 tablespoons vinegar
1 tablespoon sugar

Fry bacon until crisp. Drain the grease and save 1 tablespoon in the skillet. Sauté the onion in the reserved bacon drippings until tender. Add the green beans, vinegar, and sugar. Cover and cook over medium heat until hot, stirring occasionally.

Serves 6 to 8.

DILLED POTATOES

¼ cup olive or canola oil
1 pound red new potatoes, cut in half
3 tablespoons vinegar
3 tablespoons fresh dill, minced
salt and pepper to taste

In a skillet, warm the oil over medium heat. Add the potatoes and sauté, stirring frequently for 15 minutes or until lightly brown and tender. Add the vinegar and cook for another 5 minutes. Sprinkle with fresh dill and season with salt and pepper.

Serves 4 to 6.

BAKED BEANS

½ pound dry pinto beans
2 tablespoons olive or canola oil
1 large onion, chopped
2 cloves garlic, minced
1 jalapeño pepper, cored, seeded, and minced
1 tablespoon ginger
1½ cups apple cider or apple juice
½ cup vinegar
3 tablespoons molasses
3 tablespoons brown sugar
1 bay leaf
1 tablespoon thyme
salt and pepper to taste

1. Rinse the beans and place them in a large bowl. Cover with cold water and let them soak overnight. In the morning, drain the beans and place them in a glass or other nonmetal ovenproof casserole dish.
2. Preheat the oven to 350 degrees.
3. In a skillet, warm the oil over medium heat. Add the onion, garlic, and jalapeño pepper. Sauté for about 5 minutes or until the onion is limp, stirring occasionally. Stir the mixture into the beans and add the remaining ingredients. Cover, and bake 2 to 3 hours or until the beans are tender.

Serves 6 to 8.

■ Breads ■

MOM'S SPECIAL VINEGAR MILK BISCUITS

4 tablespoons vinegar
¾ cup sweet milk
1¾ cup all-purpose flour
¾ teaspoon salt
½ teaspoon baking soda
2 teaspoons baking powder
3 tablespoons cooking oil

1. Preheat the oven to 450 degrees.
2. Line a countertop with waxed paper and sprinkle it with flour.
3. In a small bowl, add the vinegar to the milk; set aside.
4. In a medium-size bowl, sift the flour, salt, baking soda, and baking powder together. Add cooking oil and the milk mixture. Beat hard with a spoon until the consistency is even.
5. Turn the batter out onto the waxed paper. Knead the dough lightly about 20 to 25 times, about ½ minute. Pat the dough out to ½-inch thickness.
6. Cut out biscuits and put them in a well-greased pan 2 inches apart. Grease the tops with cooking oil.
7. Bake the biscuits for 10 minutes. Reduce the heat to 400 degrees and bake until golden brown, about 10 more minutes.

Makes 6 to 12 biscuits.

STICKY CARAMEL ROLLS

2 packages dry active yeast
½ cup lukewarm water
1½ cup lukewarm milk
½ cup sugar
2 teaspoons salt
2 eggs
½ cup soft shortening or oil
7 cups flour
¼ cup brown sugar
1 tablespoon vinegar
4 tablespoons water
4 tablespoons corn syrup
½ cup butter
1 teaspoon vanilla

1. In a small bowl, combine the yeast and warm water; set aside for 15 minutes.
2. In a medium-size bowl, combine the milk, sugar, and salt and add the yeast mixture. Add the eggs, shortening or oil, and 6 cups flour, reserving 1 cup of the flour for later, if necessary. Stir until the consistency is even.
3. Remove the dough to a lightly floured board and knead for 15 to 20 minutes. The dough should remain somewhat sticky and elastic.
4. Pat the dough into a floured ball and let it rise to double its size, then punch down. Let it rise again to double its size, then roll it out on a board into a rectangle ½- to ¾-inch thick.
5. Sprinkle it with brown sugar, then roll it up like a jelly roll. Preheat the oven to 375 degrees.
6. In a small saucepan, bring the brown sugar, vinegar, water, corn syrup, butter, and vanilla to a boil. Boil it for about one minute, until it foams. Put the saucepan in a water bath to cool.

7. Slice the rolls 1 to 2 inches thick and place on a baking pan close together. Let rise for 30 minutes. Bake for 20 to 30 minutes or until done.

Makes 3 dozen.

■ Desserts ■

VINEGAR PASTRY (PIE CRUST)

This pie crust can be used unbaked for fruit pies and other cooked recipes, or you can bake the pastry for cream pies that do not require baking.

> *3 cups flour*
> *1 cup shortening*
> *½ teaspoon salt*
> *1 egg*
> *5 tablespoons cold water*
> *1 tablespoon white vinegar*

1. Preheat the oven to 425 degrees.
2. In a large bowl, mix the flour, shortening, and salt with a pastry blender until you have fine crumbs about the size of small peas.
3. In a separate bowl, beat the egg with a fork. Add cold water and vinegar and stir to combine.
4. Add the liquid to the flour mixture until thoroughly blended.
5. Divide the dough into 3 balls of equal size. Each ball makes one single 9-inch pastry.
6. Roll each ball of dough out until it is large enough to cover the pie pan. Place the dough into the pan and trim the overhanging edge of the pastry 1 inch from the rim. Use a fork to flatten the pastry evenly on the rim of the pie pan. Prick the bottom and sides thoroughly with a fork.

7. If you want to use the crust for a cream pie, bake the crust in the oven until lightly brown for about 8 to 10 minutes.

NOTE: If wrapped in plastic wrap, the extra dough can be stored in the refrigerator for 2 weeks. Remove dough from refrigerator several hours before rolling out. Any extra dough can also be frozen up to 6 months.

PEACH PIE

Adding vinegar to the dough affects the gluten in the flour and produces a tender, light, and flaky crust.

CRUST INGREDIENTS
¼ cup cold water
yolk from 1 large egg (reserve egg white)
1 tablespoon cider vinegar
2 cups all-purpose flour
1 stick (½ cup), plus 2 tablespoons cold butter or margarine (not spread), cut in small pieces

FILLING INGREDIENTS
3 pounds (about 9 medium-size) ripe peaches
1 cup granulated sugar, plus ¼ cup granulated sugar for top of crust
3 tablespoons all-purpose flour
1 tablespoon vinegar
2 tablespoons butter or margarine
reserved egg white mixed with 2 teaspoons water

To prepare the crust:
1. In a small bowl, mix the water, yolk, and vinegar until blended.
2. Put the flour in a medium-size bowl. Cut in the butter or margarine with a pastry blender or two knives until the mix-

ture resembles coarse crumbs. Stir in the water mixture with a fork until crumbs clump together to form a dough.

3. Gather the dough into a ball, divide it in half, flatten each half into a disk, and wrap it in waxed paper. Refrigerate for 30 minutes or until firm enough to roll out.

To prepare the filling:
1. Peel and pit the peaches and cut the flesh in ½-inch-thick wedges (about 7 cups).
2. Mix the sugar and flour in a large bowl. Add the peaches, sprinkle with vinegar, and toss until evenly coated.

To prepare the pie:
1. Heat the oven to 375 degrees.
2. On a lightly floured surface with a lightly floured rolling pin, roll out half of the refrigerated dough to a 12-inch circle. Fit the circle of dough into a 9-inch pie plate.
3. Spoon the peach filling into the unbaked pie shell and dot with butter or margarine.
4. Roll the remaining dough into a 10-inch circle. Cut with a pastry wheel or sharp knife into twelve ¾-inch-wide strips. Arrange 6 strips across the filling, using the longest for the center. Lay the remaining strips on top in the opposite direction, weaving them under the bottom strips, if desired. Trim the ends to the inner edge of the pie plate. Press the ends of the dough strips to the edge of the bottom crust. Roll the overhang of the bottom crust up over the edges of strips to form an even rim. Flute or crimp the edge. Brush the lattice with the egg-white mixture, then sprinkle with sugar.
5. Bake 50 to 55 minutes, until pastry is golden brown and peaches are tender when pierced. Cool on a wire rack for at least 1 hour before serving.

Serves 6 to 8.

VINEGAR PIE

½ cup margarine, melted and cooled
3 eggs, slightly beaten
¼ cup vinegar
1¼ cups sugar
2 tablespoons flour
1 tablespoon vanilla
9-inch pie shell (frozen, or use Vinegar Pastry recipe)

1. Preheat the oven to 325 degrees.
2. In a large bowl, mix the margarine, eggs, vinegar, sugar, flour, and vanilla until well blended. Pour this mixture into the unbaked pie shell.
3. Bake the pie for about 1 hour. Check it a few minutes before the hour. The filling is light brown when the pie is done.
4. Allow the pie to cool before cutting it into slices. It is delicious cold or warmed up in the microwave.

Serves 6 to 8.

WACKY VINEGAR CAKE

1 teaspoon baking soda
1 cup sugar
2 tablespoons cocoa
½ cup flour
¼ teaspoon salt
1 tablespoon vinegar
1 tablespoon vanilla
1 tablespoon cooking oil
1 cup water
powdered sugar or frosting

1. Preheat the oven to 350 degrees.
2. In a large bowl, mix the baking soda, sugar, cocoa, flour, and salt together. Sift the mixture into an 8″ x 8″ cake pan.

3. Make 3 holes in the mixture and pour the vinegar, vanilla, and cooking oil into the holes, separately.
4. Pour the water over the whole mixture, then mix until lumps are gone. Bake for 30 to 35 minutes or until a toothpick comes out clean.
5. Sprinkle powdered sugar on top or frost.

Serves 6 to 9.

FRUIT VINEGAR CAKE

3 tablespoons vinegar
1 cup milk
1 teaspoon baking soda
¾ cup butter or margarine
¾ cup brown sugar
1 cup plus 2 tablespoons flour
1 cup candied cherries
1 cup candied pineapples or mixed fruit
1 teaspoon cinnamon

1. Preheat the oven to 350 degrees. Grease an 8″ x 8″ pan.
2. In a large bowl, stir the vinegar into the milk; add the baking soda and stir.
3. In a separate bowl, cream the butter or margarine, sugar, and flour together. Add the fruit and cinnamon and stir. Fold in the milk mixture and beat well.
4. Pour the batter into the pan and bake for 1 hour.

Serves 9 to 12.

Sugar Crisp Cookies

Don't let the vinegar in this recipe scare you. These cookies are light and crisp, and they taste wonderful. They are done when they turn a light golden brown.

> ½ cup margarine, softened
> ¾ cup sugar
> 1¾ cups flour
> 1 teaspoon baking soda
> 2 teaspoons vinegar
> 1 teaspoon vanilla

1. Preheat the oven to 350 degrees.
2. In a small bowl, cream the margarine and sugar together. Sift the flour and baking soda into the creamed mixture. Add the vinegar and vanilla and stir until the consistency is even.
3. Drop the batter by rounded teaspoons onto an ungreased cookie sheet.
4. Bake 12 to 15 minutes.

Makes about 5 dozen cookies.

Easy Brownies

> 3 cups flour
> 2 cups sugar
> 2 teaspoons baking soda
> 1 teaspoon salt
> ½ cup cocoa
> 2 tablespoons vinegar
> 2 teaspoons vanilla
> ⅔ cup cooking oil
> 2 cups cold water
> ½ cups chopped nuts, if desired

1. Preheat the oven to 350 degrees.

2. In a large mixing bowl, mix the dry ingredients together. Make 3 holes in the mixture and pour the vinegar, vanilla, and cooking oil into the holes, separately. Pour the water over the whole mixture, then mix until the lumps are gone.

3. Pour the mixture into a 9″ x 13″ pan. Bake for 25 to 30 minutes or until a toothpick comes out clean.

Serves 16 to 24.

SNOW-WHITE FROSTING

This frosting is perfect for cakes or brownies.

> *whites from 2 large eggs*
> *1 cup sugar*
> *2 tablespoons water*
> *1 tablespoon light corn syrup*
> *½ teaspoon white vinegar*
> *¾ teaspoon vanilla extract*
> *2 to 3 drops almond extract*

1. Place the egg whites, sugar, water, corn syrup, and vinegar in the top of a double boiler.

2. Beat the mixture with a handheld electric mixer on high speed 7 minutes or until semifirm peaks form when beaters are lifted.

3. Remove the frosting from the heat; beat in the vanilla and almond extracts.

Frosts 2 layers or 24 cupcakes.

OLD-FASHIONED HARD CANDY

2 cups sugar
½ cup vinegar
2 tablespoons butter

1. Grease a large cookie sheet.
2. In a saucepan, mix the sugar, vinegar, and butter together. Cook over medium-high heat until the mixture starts to boil. Continue cooking, stirring frequently, to 270 degrees on a candy thermometer (or until a few drops of the mixture dropped into very cold water separates into threads that are hard).
3. Pour the mixture onto the cookie sheet and cut into 1-inch squares while the candy is still warm. When the candy is cool enough to handle, roll squares into balls with hands.
4. If desired, you can add a few drops of your favorite flavoring or extract and a few drops of food coloring. Add peppermint, cherry, or lemon extract, and you have homemade cough drops.

Makes about 50 candies.

VINEGAR TAFFY

1 cup sugar
2 cups dark corn syrup
2 tablespoons butter
1 tablespoon vinegar
¼ teaspoon baking soda
1 teaspoon vanilla

1. Combine the sugar, syrup, butter, and vinegar in a saucepan. Bring to a boil over medium heat, stirring constantly until sugar is dissolved.
2. Continue cooking to the hard-ball stage (a small amount of

candy dropped into cold water forms a hard ball), then remove from the heat and stir in the baking soda and vanilla.
3. Beat the mixture by hand until smooth and creamy, then pour it into an 8″ x 8″ buttered pan.
4. When cool enough to handle, pull the batter with your fingers until the candy is satiny and light colored. Pull into long strips and cut into desired lengths.
5. Wrap pieces in waxed paper and store in an airtight container.

Makes about 1 pound.

VINEGAR AND MOLASSES TAFFY

This recipe dates back to the Roaring Twenties!

2 cups molasses
1 cup white sugar
1 tablespoon butter
1 teaspoon vinegar

1. Combine all the ingredients in a saucepan and boil for 20 minutes, stirring constantly.
2. Beat the mixture by hand until smooth and creamy, then pour it into an 8″ x 8″ buttered pan.
3. When cool enough to handle, pull the batter with your fingers until the candy is satiny and light colored. Pull into long strips and cut into desired lengths.
4. Wrap pieces in waxed paper and store in an airtight container.

Makes about 1 pound.

SPONGE CANDY

This is a light-textured candy that can be dipped in chocolate if desired.

> *1 cup sugar*
> *1 cup dark corn syrup*
> *1 tablespoon distilled white vinegar*
> *1 tablespoon baking soda*

1. Line a square 8″ x 8″ cake pan with foil on the bottom and sides, extending it over the edges. Butter the foil.
2. Mix the sugar, syrup, and vinegar in a saucepan over medium heat. Continue to cook until candy thermometer reaches 300 degrees, stirring occasionally. Turn off the heat and add baking soda immediately. Stir until well mixed. The baking soda will cause the mixture to start foaming. Pour the mixture into the greased pan while it is still foaming.
3. Let the candy cool completely. When cool, lift the candy out of pan and break into bite-size pieces. Store in an airtight container.

■ Snacks ■

BEEF JERKY

> *1 pound lean beef (chuck or round)*
> *¼ cup Worcestershire sauce*
> *¼ cup soy sauce*
> *1 tablespoon tomato sauce*
> *1 tablespoon vinegar*
> *1 teaspoon sugar*
> *¼ teaspoon onion powder*
> *1 teaspoon salt*
> *¼ teaspoon garlic powder*

1. Trim all visible fat from the lean beef and freeze until firm enough to cut into slices. Use a sharp knife to cut into very thin slices. Cut across the grain and make the slices as thin as possible, ⅛ inch or less.
2. Cut the slices into 1-inch wide strips. Arrange strips in a baking pan.
3. In a bowl combine the remaining ingredients and stir well. Pour this liquid over the meat strips. Refrigerate overnight.
4. Preheat the oven to 140 degrees.
5. Remove the meat from the marinade and place the strips on a cake rack over a cookie sheet in the oven. Strips will splinter on the edges when done. It generally takes 18 to 24 hours, depending on how thin you cut the pieces. Cool completely before wrapping with plastic wrap. Jerky will keep in a closely covered container for 2 to 4 weeks.

▪ Drinks ▪

HAYMAKER'S DRINK (A THIRST QUENCHER)

In the old days (before Gatorade) this was a popular thirst quencher. Farmers working in the fields drank this by the gallon.

1 gallon water
1 cup molasses
1¼ cups vinegar
2 cups sugar
1 teaspoon ginger

Mix all ingredients and serve chilled or over ice.

Serves 16 to 24.

HEALTHY THIRST QUENCHER

This is an old folk remedy that is said to cure everything from arthritis to high blood pressure to memory loss.

> *1 tablespoon cider vinegar*
> *1 tablespoon honey*
> *1 glass cold water*

Mix together and drink.

Serves 1.

POWER JUICE

This is a favorite energy booster for runners and other athletes.

> *8 ounces apple juice*
> *2 ounces grape juice*
> *1 tablespoon apple cider vinegar*

Mix together and chill. Drink 2 portions daily.

Serves 1.

SUMMERTIME BERRY FIZZ

This is a wonderful summertime drink.

> *4 cups strawberries, blueberries, or raspberries*
> *1 cup white vinegar*
> *2 cups sugar*

Place 2 cups of the berries in a clean glass jar and pour the vinegar over them. Stir to mix and moisten, cover the jar, and place it in a cool, dark place for at least 2 days. Strain the liquid through a double layer of cheesecloth or through a coffee filter into a clean glass jar, discarding the berries. Add the remaining 2 cups of berries to the jar, cover, and place in a cool, dark place for at least 2 days.

Strain the liquid from the second batch of berries and discard the fruit. Place the liquid in a glass or enamel saucepan. Add the sugar. Heat the juice and sugar slowly, bringing it to a boil. Continue to boil it for 20 minutes. Skim off any foam that develops as it is boiling. Cool the liquid and store it in a clean glass jar in the refrigerator.

To make a berry fizz drink, add 2 tablespoons to an 8-ounce glass of water or club soda. Add ice and a slice of fresh lemon or lime.

■ MAIL-ORDER SOURCES ■

Most of these companies will mail you a free catalog. A few may charge a small fee (such as one dollar) for the catalog that may be refundable with the first order. If you can't find the vinegar-making supplies you need locally, these resources will help you locate them.

SOURCES FOR VINEGAR-MAKING SUPPLIES, BOTTLES, AND LABELS

Aspen TypoGraphix
1648 Old Hart Ranch Road
Roseville, CA 95661
Phone (916) 786–5955
Sells: Labels for vinegar bottles; $2 catalog cost

Balducci's
424 Sixth Avenue
New York, NY 10011
Phone (800) 225–3822
Sells: Vinegars

Barrel Builders
P.O. Box 268
St. Helena, CA 94574
Phone (800) 365–8231
Sells: Barrels; call or write for a free catalog.

The Cantinetta at Tra Vigne
1050 Charter Oak Road
St. Helena, CA 94574
Phone (707) 963–8888
Sells: Crocks for making vinegar, active vinegars, and many other
vinegar-making supplies.

Chicama Vineyards
Stoney Hill Road, P.O. Box 430
West Tisbury, Martha's Vineyard, MA 02575–0430
Phone (508) 693–0309
Sells: Vinegars made from their wine; offers many flavors; call or
write for a free catalog.

Corti Brothers
5770 Freeport Boulevard
Sacramento, CA 95822
Phone (916) 736–3800
Sells: Vinegars

Napa Fermentation Supplies
P.O. Box 5839
Napa, CA 94581
Phone (707) 255–6372
Sells: 8-ounce jar of vinegar mother and vinegar-making instruc-
tions.

Sur La Table
84 Pine Street
Seattle, WA 98101
Phone (206) 448–2244
Sells: Bottles

SOURCES FOR HERB PLANTS AND SEEDS

Burpee & Company
300 Park Avenue
Warminster, PA 18974
Phone (800) 888–1447
Large selection of herb seeds, nice "A-Z" herb chart, colorful pictures, reasonably priced; call or write for free catalog.

Ferry-Morse Seeds
P.O. Box 488
Fulton, KY 42041
Phone (800) 283–3400
Large selection of herb seeds; colorful pictures in alphabetical order with growing chart and growing tips. Call for a free catalog.

Gurney's Seed & Nursery Company
Capital Street
Yankton, SD 57079
Phone (605) 665–1671 (Customer Service)
Nice selection of herbs and seasonings; colorful pictures, reasonably priced. Call or write for a free catalog.

Johnny's Selected Seeds
Foss Hill Road
Albion, ME 04910
Phone (207) 437–4301
Large selection of selected medicinal and culinary herbs and seasonings, full of colorful pictures. Call or write for free catalog.

Nichols Garden Nursery
1190 North Pacific Highway
Albany, OR 97321
Phone (541) 928–9280
Has a large assortment of hard-to-find herbs plants. Catalog also features rare seeds. Call or write for a free catalog.

Rabbit Show Farm
2880 East Highway 402
Loveland, CO 80537
Phone (970) 667–5531
Call for a free catalog.

Shepherd's Garden Seeds
30 Irene Street
Torrington, CT 06790
Phone (860) 482–3638
Large selection of seeds, plants, and supplies; also has unique imported varieties that are hard to find; reasonably priced. Call or write for a free catalog.

R. H. Shumway's Garden Guide
P.O. Box 1
Graniteville, SC 29829
Phone (803) 663–9771
Large illustrated selection of herbs, culinary supplies, and teas; many old-time varieties. Call or write for a free catalog.

Stokes Growers Guide
P.O. Box 548
Buffalo, NY 14240
Phone (716) 695–6980
Nice assortment of herbs and greens for almost any garden; reasonably priced with colorful descriptions; large or small quantities available for purchase. Call or write for a free catalog.

Thompson & Morgan, Inc.
P.O. Box 1308
Jackson, NJ 08527
Phone (908) 363–2225
Phone (800) 274–7333
Good selection of herbs and spices; colorful pictures and reasonably priced; handy-size catalog. Call or write for a free catalog.

■ REFERENCES ■

Arkin, Frieda. *Kitchen Wisdom.* New York: Galahad Books, 1993.

Bakule, Paula Drefus. *Rodale's Book of Practical Formulas.* New York: MJF Books, 1991.

Better Homes and Gardens. *Household Hints and Tips.* Des Moines: Dorling Kindersley, 1991.

Birnes, Nancy. *Cheaper & Better.* New York: Shadow Lawn Press, 1987.

Brennen, Sherri. *Better Living.* Tulsa, Okla.: Council Oak Books, 1994.

Bruun, Erik. *Household Hints and Formulas.* New York: Black Dog & Leventhal Publishers, 1994.

Chapin, Patricia. *Natural Health Remedies.* Boca Raton, Fla.: Globe Communications, 1994.

Chiarello, Michael. *Flavored Vinegars.* San Francisco: Chronicle Books, 1996.

Ciullo, Peter. *Baking Soda Bonanza.* New York: HarperPerennial, 1995.

Consumer Guide, ed. *Favorite Helpful Household Hints.* Lincolnwood, Ill.: Publications International, 1986.

Crocker, Betty (General Mills, Inc.). *Betty Crocker's Cookbook.* New York: Bantam Books, 1969.

Edwards, Pat. *Cheap Eating*. Hineburg, Vt.: Upper Access, Inc., 1993.

Family Circle. *Hints, Tips & Smart Advice*. New York: Mallard Press, 1992.

Faythimes. *Gram's Good Grub*. Amherst, Wis.:, Palmer Publications, 1992.

Florman, Monte and Marjorie. *How to Clean Practically Anything*. Yonkers, N.Y.: Consumer Reports Books, 1992.

Harris, Marjorie. *Better House and Planet*. Toronto: Key Porter Books, 1991.

Jarvis, D. C. *Folk Medicine*. New York: Fawcett Crest, 1958.

Johnson, Marsha Peters. *Gourmet Vinegars*. Lake Oswego, Ore.: Culinary Arts Ltd., 1989.

Moore, Melodie. *Skinflint News*. Palm Harbor, Fla.: Skinflint Publishing, 1989.

———. *Smart Solutions for Saving Money*. Palm Harbor, Fla.: Skinflint Publishing, 1995.

———. *The Frugal Almanac*. Lincolnwood, Ill.: Publications International, 1996.

———. *The Grocery Guide*. Palm Harbor, Fla.: Skinflint Publishing, 1994.

———. *Tightwad Living Magazine*. Palm Harbor, Fla.: Skinflint Publishing, 1989–96.

Moore, Ron and Melodie. *Smart Cents*. Los Angeles: Price, Stern, Sloan, 1993.

Oster, Maggie. *Herbal Vinegar*. Pownal, Vt.: Storey Communications, 1991.

Pinkham, Mary Ellen. *Mary Ellen's Greatest Hints*. New York: Fawcett Crest, 1990.

Proulx, Earl. *Old-Timer Tricks That Do the Impossible Around Your Home*. Dublin, N.H.: Yankee Publishing, 1993.

Quillin, Patrick. *Honey, Garlic & Vinegar Home Remedies*. North Canton, Ohio: Leader Company, 1996.

Reader's Digest Association. *Household Hints & Handy Tips*. Pleasantville, N.Y.: Reader's Digest Association, 1988.

Rodale. *Rodale's Book of Hints, Tips & Everyday Wisdom*. Emmaus, Pa.: Rodale Press, 1985.

Romanowski, Frank. *Making Vinegar at Home*. Northampton, Mass.: Beer & Winemaking Supplies, Inc., 1989.

Rosso, Julee, and Sheila Lukins. *The New Basics Cookbook.* New York: Workman Publishing, 1989.

Sally, Aunt. *Aunt Sally's Tried and True Home Remedies.* New York: Gramercy Books, 1993.

Steer, Gina. *The Gourmet Kitchen Vinegars.* Menlo Park, Calif.: Sunset Publishing Corp., 1994.

Thacker, Emily. *The Vinegar Book.* Canton, Ohio: Tresco Publishers, 1995.

Ward, Bernard. *Apple Cider Vinegar.* Boca Raton, Fla.: Globe Communications, 1995.

Wylie, Harriet. *420 Ways to Clean Everything.* New York: Wings Books, 1992.

■ KEEP IN TOUCH ■

If you have discovered a use for vinegar that is not included in this book, I invite you to send it to me, Melodie Moore, at the address below.

Melodie Moore is the editor and publisher of *Tightwad Living*, a magazine packed full of money-saving tips, household hints, low-cost recipes, and many other thrifty ideas. The magazine is published ten times a year, and you can subscribe for twelve dollars per year. Send in the coupon below for a complimentary copy.

COUPON FOR A FREE 16-PAGE
MONEY-SAVING MAGAZINE ($2.95 RETAIL VALUE)

Send this coupon and a #10 self-addressed stamped (2 stamps) envelope to:

> Tightwad Living (Dept. VB)
> 539 Kennedy Bridge Road
> Harrodsburg, KY 40330

Name _____

Street _____

City _____

State _____ Zip _____

**YES! SEND ME A FREE COPY OF
TIGHTWARD LIVING.**

■ INDEX ■